No Addict Left Behind

NO ADDICT LEFT BEHIND

It's a Recovery Medicine State of Mind

JOEY PAGANO, MSW, LSW, CRS

Co-authored by SCOTT A. COOK, MD, MPH

THE POINT BREEZE© PUBLISHING COMPANY

Proofreader: Kellie McKevitt, BS, MSW

Book Editors: Mark Chait & Amy Kirtley-Hill

Book Cover: Joey Pagano, Jodie Pagano & Oceana Garceau

Book Illustrator: Kiko Pollock

Book Publicists: Samantha Showman & Jodie Pagano

I do not endorse or promote any specific modality of recovery or treatment. This book is about accepting and loving a person where they are in their life regardless of another individual's perspective. It is with love and autonomy that I am guided. I believe we are put here on this earth to live, let live, and, most of all, be kind.

NO ADDICT LEFT BEHIND

It's a Recovery Medicine State of Mind

FIRST EDITION

ISBN   978-1-5445-4136-5 *Hardcover*

         978-1-5445-4137-2 *Paperback*

         978-1-5445-4138-9 *Ebook*

         978-1-5445-4139-6 *Audiobook*

This book is dedicated to my mother, Cindy; father, Timothy; precious wife, Jodie; son, Zavier; daughter, Gianna; sister, Samantha, and her husband, Timothy; brother, Xavier; and mother-in-law, Diane. Thank you also to those who loved me until I learned to love myself. A special shout-out to Dr. Scott A. Cook, Tyler, Kellie, Cheryld, Rita, Lee, Jason, Erika, Judy, Sam, Erin, Kiko, and George. You all taught me the true meaning of unconditional love, empathy, understanding, and, most of all, compassion. Thank you! And a big thank you to everyone who donated and helped us bring this book to life! Most importantly, prayers for our lost loved ones, the people who only stayed for parts of my journey. For those who never stuck around or were taken from this world way too early, there will always be a moment of silence for them. To the friends, acquaintances, and anybody I met through my process—I love you all! You are all my inspirations, as you are me, as I am you. Words from your heart touched my heart and unlocked my prison. I only hope that I can someday be a part of your story.

CONTENTS

PRELUDE

Dear Addiction, I love you so, so much. You are the rock to my roll, yet at the same time, I have always hated you. I am so forsaken by you; you left me to die, wither away. But see, you have made me who I am today and taught me so much. For that reason, I cannot turn my back on you because I am you; I am the disease. You have carved me out in your image. I am sincerely grateful, yet at times so, so mad. The truth is that I once was so lost, but now I am found. My spirit and soul were hiding under a mask that left me to die, but as I stumbled, you picked me up again and again. You didn't leave this addict behind.

"June 1, 2013—Every End Has a Beginning"

INTRODUCTION

When all you have left in life is hope, it is just enough for a new beginning.

The clock ticked nine as I walked into work. I couldn't believe it had been almost ten years since I got clean; it felt like only a few days to me at that moment. As I looked at the calendar on my wall, there was an inscription on the current date stating, "Sometimes good things have to end for wonderful things to begin." I put my head down and chuckled to myself. Today, I felt simply grateful. Although I was still smiling, a chill ran down my spine as I looked at the diplomas I had hung on my wall.

I turned my head to the door as a loud bang rang out, as my first client rushed into my office with a sense of urgency.

She yelled my name and seemed to be crying. "Please help me, Joey!" she called out, sweat streaming down her face. "Please don't give up on me; I'm such a failure. I can't get this right; I think I might give up."

I looked her straight in the eyes and said, "There are no failures, just delayed successes." She still could not manage to smile, though she tried. I hugged her tight as her hands dug into my back, and she did not want to let go. She grabbed my hand, and as her sweat ran down my hand, I dissociated and was somewhere else...

Will this madness ever stop? "Please, God, just let me die; I'm sick of...of...existing. KILL ME...PLEASE!" I can hear the rain gush through a crack in the ceiling of the abandoned house I call home. As sweat pours down my face, it is so cold, even though I'm wearing a hoodie and a long-sleeve shirt. I am still freezing, yet it is eighty-five degrees out. I hadn't eaten in weeks, barely surviving; my mind was lost.

I looked in the mirror and said, "Man, you look good; you lost weight, Joey." My hygiene was only a pipe dream and just not a priority...not in my hell. In my addiction, I realized that hell wasn't just a place we go, but rather my life at the moment. It had also become a distorted comfort in those days. The sad thing is I don't remember telling my teachers and family as a kid, "When I grow up, I want to be a junkie." I had dreams when I was young, but those dreams turned into tears that I kept locked inside. But God hears the tears that I won't cry.

My disease muttered to me, "Joey, you know what to do! You are not going to be dope sick today! You need to suit up and march! Get one more, Joey, just ONE MORE!"

The only thing that fed my hunger was *one more*, and that *one more* was never enough! NEVER! How would I escape the reality I lived in when there was no hope? In a world where stigma and dogma had shaped the ideology of addiction treatment, I was lost without hope. Even if I had to go through people…it had to be done. My mind raced as I went through my phone, trying to figure out what to do to get my fix to make it through the night and function normally. Yes, I said it—to *feel normal!* One thing is for sure when the grips of addiction have you: the grips OWN you. Period!

I looked out the window and yelled, "Please help!" as the sun rose and the birds chirped. That was a sound that irritated me so much! It was the sound of life and joy; I did not have time for those things. Once addiction takes you, it owns you. It gives the orders and runs the show. There are no holidays, birthdays, work, or stability in addiction. There is not any time for that. I was stuck in a vicious cycle, and some days, I would dream of being able to sleep, but it was only a distant wish. The reality is that on days like this, promises were *never kept* when the drugs and the money ran out. You can't serve two masters in addiction.

I slowly opened my eyes, took a deep breath, and noticed I was still hugging my client.

We separated, and my client looked at me and was able to smile as she sat down. I wiped the sweat off my face, as now I could think clearly. She said, "Where did you go?"

I said that I went to a place we both know so well. At that moment, we knew that words from the heart touch the heart.

For me, insane *was* sane! That was normal to me. For so many who can empathize with this story, let these words feed you.

This journey of hope was built on hard-won experiences, overcoming the stigma of addiction, and realizing that our struggles do not define us but refine us into who we are today.

As the clock struck five, I grabbed my coat and felt like I could breathe better, knowing I was done for the day. I slowly walked out of my office, smiling as I closed the door. Today was a great day, even though it was a stressor. Sitting back in my car, I closed my eyes and prayed. I was grateful that I was still clean and knew I was right where I belonged. I had to remain in the trenches, fighting the disease of addiction while it took the lives of so many. This was a war where addiction's biggest weapons are the stigma and dogma of our world. I am free to be myself today, and that gift is priceless.

June 1, 2013, is a day I will keep locked in my heart forever, for it is my clean date. My name is Joey Pagano, and I am a licensed social worker, therapist, supervisor, and, most of all, recovering addict. Each chapter in the book contains experiences, with each moment of them holding a special meaning in my life.

I want to take you on this journey and let you see the world through my experiences. While I reflect on various points in my life, you will view my life with your eyes.

Not only do I want to talk about my personal experiences, but also Dr. Scott A. Cook and I will relate my experiences with clinical perspectives that shed light on the array of solutions in recovery medicine. Recovery is not the same for everyone; it is individualized, just as the experiences in my life have been.

Occasionally, I have flashbacks that take me back to places I do not want to return to. The flashbacks keep me locked up in my feelings, which help me and hurt me. This was a day just like that. My life was built from similar hard-won experiences. It all started from living in a world filled with stigma and hoping to one day not be judged by another person's creed.

Chapter 1

YOU DO IT THIS WAY, OR YOU AREN'T THAT!

One of the hardest parts of recovery is stigma, and with that comes the directives of the masses who are sure they have the right answer. Sharing stories of these struggles is an important part of the journey.

We always want something to be done our way; if it's not done our way, it must be wrong. Whether it is the stigma or dogma that comes with addiction, these thoughts can kill a person.

It was a time when I had five months clean, and my life seemed dictated by how I had to recover.

My disease yelled to get my attention. "You need to do it this way, Joey! Any other way is just not good enough! You will fail!" That comment was why I kept failing for decades. As I held my head in shame, my mind would not shut off. "Why even try, Joey? Just give up!"

The dogma of those early recovery internal conversations was nothing but a rigid, unbending doctrine that addiction kept locked in there.

All I could ever hear in my head was, "You do it this way, or you aren't that!"

Our country is a place that has been built on letting others tell us what we can and can't do. The unrealistic expectations we put on our loved ones keep us locked in the same chains of the dogma of what others want us to be. I spent years in the chains, trapped, with the key to escape buried in my pocket. I couldn't pull it out.

Prior to my getting clean, I remember conversing with my father, who looked at me with disgust and sadness while hoping I would just quit using. I would look at him and say, "I can get clean *any* day I want, as long as it's not *today*."

That statement would ring true to an addict, but I knew my father would never understand. For persons in addiction, that day might never come. Today is only a dream for some addicts. Some never even receive the first chance at a life of recovery. With a mind fueled with prejudices, a person might never break free from those chains.

Stigma can be defined as "a mark of disgrace associated with a particular circumstance, quality, or person." To a person in recovery, it is a line drawn in your thoughts and actions that screams, "You shall not pass!"

I ask myself daily, "How do we as a nation play God and pass judgment on persons we know nothing about?" Or I ask this question: "How do we know the right path for one person is the best for another?"

We can make our best clinical decision, but there is no cookie-cutter process regarding recovery treatment. Stigma will keep me trapped in a dark place, where I feel that there is no way out. Recovery medicine has become a scope of human services where the seeds of stigma have continued to bloom from a practitioner's implicit biases.

The seeds of addiction are sometimes planted very young and seem to grow from questions from our loved ones, asking, "Why can't you just quit using?" If a practitioner can meet a client where the client is and not where they are, the seeds of hope can be grown instead. In the world of addiction and recovery, some seeds grow without any watering at all.

Ask yourself this question: "If addiction is a disease, just like any other, how can we take away someone's autonomy, create a doctrine of our own, clinical or spiritual, and force others to live by our values?"

If we cultivate the client by prostituting our belief system to them, we put that person back into the same dark corner they hid in for years. This is the same dark corner where the stigma of our country's healthcare system has sent many people to their graves.

* * *

I learned that stigma can hold a veteran hostage in a prison where the door locks from the inside. The key was always in my pocket, but I never had the strength to let myself out. I will never forget the day when stigma shook this veteran's prison door, and I hung my head even lower. It was a beautiful Sunday, with the sun shining as we went on a family outing. We were listening to music and trying to find a parking space at Lowe's Plaza. My wife, Jodie, looked around and saw the "veterans only" parking spot.

My smile disappeared as I heard the words slowly emerge from Jodie's mouth. "Hey, park there, Joey," she said.

With a sigh, I responded, "I can't, babe. I am not a veteran." I bowed my head and sweat began to run down my face. I felt in my gut as if someone had just punched me.

Jodie looked back at me; her hand was now on my shoulder. Her face blushed as she spoke louder. "Yes, you are." The truth was that I felt less than a veteran.

While I looked at that parking spot, it was as if I could hear the voice of my platoon sergeant still yelling at me in anger, "You are an addict and we do not tolerate addicts around here." Those words crippled me, as they ran through my mind repeatedly.

In 1996, I was discharged from the army, stigmatized, not given the option to enter treatment, and labeled a junkie. I was given a general with other than honorable (OTH) discharge, with no hope in sight. To a veteran, this was a scarlet letter, a mark that would never go away and damage me for the rest of my life. I was in the US Army and couldn't stop using drugs. I had a disease but did not know I had a disease. The army's cure was to get rid of me and send me back home without any treatment.

I still get flashbacks from those moments, throwing me back and reminding me of that dark place.

I can still hear the sergeant yelling at me. "Private, you are getting discharged now. You will never come back on this base. We do not want any addicts around here! I am going to drop you off on the interstate, and you'll never see me again."

They called me a junkie, an addict, and it was a time when I did not understand that I suffered from a disease. I did not know there was treatment, let alone what treatment even consisted of. All I knew was that I was suffering, and now there was no way out. I was going back to the dark corner I came from. The stigma ran deep if you were an addict in the military in the 1990s.

My wife asked me to tell her the story; she had only ever heard bits and pieces at different times. I looked at her and said, "I'll tell you what happened. It may help me. I guess that pain shared is pain lessened."

* * *

"Dear, it was the day of my army discharge, and I was emotionless." Chills were rushing down my spine as I spoke those words. "I was riding in the Humvee with the platoon sergeant, who kept his words short with me and did his best to rush me through this process. We reached the I-5 interstate near Seattle, Washington, and the vehicle stopped suddenly. The staff sergeant looked me in the eyes, and I felt his stare piercing my soul.

I looked up at him, knowing it was time to leave. He yelled,

"Get out of the Humvee!" I grabbed the only thing I owned, my duffle bag, as my feet hit the street while jumping out of the Humvee on I-5.

I was distraught, tired, and anxious, not knowing what life had in store for me. I was trying to hurry up because the staff sergeant's facial expression told me that he did not have time. I was an inconvenience to him.

I started to walk down I-5 while the sergeant looked at me and said, "Be happy I took you this far. I only had to take you to the boundary of the base."

I was a scared twenty-year-old addict who was lost and had to walk to Seattle from Ft. Lewis, which was thirty miles away. The only way to get to the airport was to walk or hitchhike, and I knew it. I put my head down and slowly walked down the interstate with sweat running down my face. I was tired and felt like a failure. I did not understand what addiction was, but it had me in its grips and wasn't letting me go. I was a person who did not know there was a way out or that I was an addict. I had no knowledge of recovery and no idea what I should do.

I was stigmatized, and my dream of being a soldier was lost to addiction. The construct of the military had me on a one-way ticket home with the seeds of addiction planted. These seeds were being cultivated by stigma, dogma, and other attitudes that would set me on a path to destruction. To me, all hope was gone.

* * *

"Joey, I see why that story still haunts you," my wife uttered as tears ran down my face.

I slowly walked away from her and kept walking until I reached the veterans sign. I reached out my hand and touched the parking sign, saying, "Maybe one day I'll feel more like a vet, but that day is not today."

The stigma of a veteran in recovery cut like a knife, and the wounds still felt fresh in my heart. And those wounds might never go away. Each time I think I am over something, it comes back tenfold.

These wounds felt like battle scars from active addiction. I did not know how many battles I would have to fight through to make it to the other side.

Stigma is a monster that continues to terrorize a person and leaves claw marks all over a person's spirit. All it ever does is change shape from one experience to another. Living as a veteran and an addict is a tough pill to swallow. The only thing that makes it go down smoother is the empathy and compassion of another person who can share their story. Just as the stigma of a veteran stings, the struggles of a recovering addict do not let up.

Walking into an emergency room was just as bad as seeing the veteran parking sign. It was the same sting, just a different scar. In 2007, in one of my many opioid overdoses, I was taken to the ER to be stabilized. This is a memory of the stigma of an addict I will never forget.

This memory cannot be erased or changed; I can only learn

from this experience. And it comes alive every time I walk into the ER.

This was a dark moment in my life, and death almost had its grip on me. It was 1:30 a.m., and I could barely see the clock with my eyes wanting to stay shut. I kept nodding out as I tried my best to raise my head. I slowly lifted my head and yelled, "Where am I?" Several people were dressed in scrubs in my room, with one trying to put an IV in my arm.

The nurse spoke loudly. "Keep your arms still, sir." She looked at the phlebotomist and said, "You try. I can't stick him."

Looking back at the nurse, she smirked and said, "Addicts are the worst to stick." The nurse and phlebotomist were exhausted and seemed to be at their wit's end with me. The room was edgy and full of tension.

Finally, my eyes opened, and I spoke loudly, saying, "I'm in the hospital. Wait, how?" They had me hooked up to several life-saving devices, and I felt so horrible, with my body still shaking. I yelled, "It is so freezing in here!"

"Sir, quiet down!" said the nurse, looking disgusted while the doctor talked to me. I glanced over at the table and saw three open Narcan packets.

I started sweating even more and yelled frantically to everyone in the room, "Did I overdose?"

The room echoed with multiple people all saying, "What?" The doctor nodded his head yes, along with the rest of the staff.

They all walked out of the room, and I was left with myself and my addiction going to work on me.

My mind was racing and would not shut off. The sweat kept pouring down my face, yet it was freezing in the room. The curtain was closed, but I listened to the staff talk about me outside the room.

The physician said with disdain, "I can't believe he is still alive. Damn junkies, they'll never learn."

The nurse agreed, chiming in, "This is getting so old; they should use the Narcan only on the addicts who want it and are willing to change."

The paramedic answered, "Yeah, this guy obviously doesn't want it."

I heard their voices, and the comment "who want it" stuck in my head. I knew that part of me wanted to be clean, but my addiction still ran the show. My disease gave the orders, and I kept showing up for duty every day.

In the ER, the stigma of an addict was real; it was a knife that would cut deep. The ER also had its own dogma, which left persons who would overdose a fate of their own.

As human beings, do we really need to ask ourselves, "Why help an addict?" We live in the real world, where there is real stigma. There is no such thing as grace in an ER for an addict.

I lay there in bed, about to give up on life, trying my best to hold on but not knowing how. I did not stay clean that day or go to treatment, but I knew that an ER was no place for an addict, no place to find a way out. I was sent back to that same dark corner once again. I was still a human being who had a desire to be clean. I didn't have the strength to make the decision yet. My mind was filled with the stigma of "once a junkie, always a junkie." I needed to hang on, get out of that corner, and not get left behind.

This memory still haunts me today. The phrase "damn junkies" sometimes keeps me locked in bondage. That day was a nightmare; if looks could kill, they would have been lethal.

Throughout my life, experiences with the stigma of addiction shaped my belief system. Through perseverance, I had to see what my recovery was worth.

Chapter 2

ADDICTION COMES IN MANY FORMS, BUT ALL END THE SAME

Like the battle scars that stigma and dogma created in my life, the many forms of addiction hit me ever so hard. The sad thing was that though they took on many forms, they all ended the same. I remember being in early recovery, having over nine months clean, and being excited to get busy living. It was morning, and I was sitting on the steps of my house when a homeless man walked by me and stopped. He was dressed in clothes that did not fit him, and he was covered in dirt. He was sweating profusely while struggling to get a word out.

He looked me in the eyes and said, "Hey, don't I know you? I saw you before somewhere. Yes, it is you! You are the guy who lived in the abandoned house with me a few years back."

As the words came out of his mouth, I answered, "Yes, that was me; I'm not that guy anymore. I got clean." I grabbed his hand and said, "You can get clean too. You don't have to live like that anymore. I believe in you."

He got down on one knee, and tears began to flow. He whispered to me, "What is your recovery worth, Joey?"

I responded with emphasis, "Everything."

The man left and I got back up and went into the house. This was a decisive moment, and I lay down on my bed to relax and try to let this moment sink in. As I drifted off to sleep, I focused on what my recovery was worth.

If someone made me an offer that I could have *anything* in the world in exchange for my clean date, would I run with that offer? Would I even consider it? Would it at least make me curious about what the offer was? Anything...Honestly? Questions like that make me think. What I'm asking is, can my recovery be bought? Whether that proposition were to include my kid's happiness, money, property, or prestige, the heart of the offer would take away my spirit, my soul, my serenity, and, eventually, my life.

If my clean date could be bought, I might have to ask myself why. What do I not see in my life, and what I am missing? Do I have a passion for my recovery? Have I found a purpose in my life? Living in recovery and having a life on the side has worked for me. I tried having a life and doing recovery on the side; heh, that path always leads to disaster, *always*! Having a purpose is certainly not restricted to my recovery either. Recovery is a lifestyle that gives me a purpose by serving others. It is the way I want to live.

I always see those people who can go through life without a purpose. I was once one of them. How did I survive that long? I numbed the pain so much that it was worse when I did feel it. I remember being so far on the edge that a little feeling left me falling into the grips of addiction. If someone asked me, in the beginning, what I would have traded my clean date for, I would have said, "Whatever, I'll get clean again. What's to offer?" This is because I was used to always giving up so fast. I constantly looked at how far I had to go instead of how far I had come. But I have faith today; my heart sees the light when my eyes only see the darkness. I'm not blind, for I can see that the world is full of a lack of trust in anything.

I do not live there today. If I go out and look for the sickness, I'll find it wherever I go, anywhere! I often see people who have lost conviction in *any* meaning at all in the world. I remember days of merely existing and taking up space, even before the grips got hold of me. See, recovery would not work like that; I battled it and lost many times. I used to not want to be found and had completely given up, but I did not realize that my breakthrough was right around the corner.

That's the miracle—sitting on my hands and finding purpose in myself. I was never promised it, but through perseverance, I got it. My heart speaks empathy today; I can feel for people because I need those hearts as they need me. Years ago, they *were* me, a shell of a spirit floating through life stuck in a void with no purpose or worth. It's empathy that connects us. But what I feel now is a proven fact: "My hope is wishing, my trust is believing, and my faith knows that as long as I don't use, it's going to be all right. Something bigger than me is at work here." The proof is there if I open my eyes and look.

I feel that I started to wake up as I realized how my life had been changing. I grew into the person I was made to be instead of the person I thought I needed to be. I was choosing life while feeling as though I was now chosen with a purpose.

For so many years, I did not know I was an addict. My parents used to take me to one psychiatric hospital after another, trying to fix me. It took such a long time to realize I wasn't broke; I just needed to be repaired. I had to understand how addiction was more than just drugs.

I used to say, "The only thing that has changed since I came into recovery is the contents of my bag." This is a powerful, valid statement. I thought life would be fine if I could just put down the substance. That was never the case, and it took me numerous "bitter ends" to see how they all resulted in the same fate.

There would be days when I would talk to my mother about addiction, but she never understood. She could not conceptualize how, as my life worsened, I still would not quit. I tried to explain how an addict's mind worked, but she could not fully grasp the concept. One day, I grabbed my mother's hand, sat down, and said to her, "Mom, let me show you what it is like to be an addict. See, it's not about the drug, for addiction will take you in many ways. Addiction comes in many forms, but the ends are always the same." I then sat back and said, "Mom, let me tell you some stories." I hoped these would give her some tangible examples.

"Mom, as I tell you this, picture these moments."

✳ ✳ ✳

The man slowly walks down the steps of his house, tiptoeing so no one hears him. He is looking for more food to cover up some feelings, which he can escape if he eats enough to wash away his pain. Sweat pours down his face as he chews his food, crouching down and trying not to make a sound.

The man whispers to himself, "As long as no one can see me, I'll be okay. Nobody must know! *Nobody!*" Though, the thing that he did not realize was that he knew.

In another story, a person stood in line at a store, needing to buy more items, but could not afford anything they were purchasing. If they bought these items, some of their bills would go unpaid. But this did not matter because the person *could not stop*. Addiction had them in its grips and would not let go. They were obsessed and compelled to suit up and march to the beat of the disease of addiction. Nothing mattered, nothing at all! These moments took away their feelings and stopped the pain for a short time. But moments don't last forever in addiction. These feelings would continue to show up for duty in the morning. You can't solve a problem by creating an additional problem. Addiction is addiction, whether it is alcohol, sex, cigarettes, caffeine, work, gambling, or drugs. Anything habit-forming, it all ends the same. It all ends in destruction.

* * *

As I told those stories, my mother's eyes widened, and I could tell she was intrigued. I continued to talk to her, hoping she would gain some understanding.

"Mom, I see people make their addictions their god; I know I did. Anything that I pick up, I will get addicted to, whether it's drugs, relationships, money, property, or prestige. I thought these things wouldn't interfere with managing my life. The truth is if you're taking out a mortgage on Amazon, setting up a payment plan for food, or going from relationship to relationship, saying, 'Well, if they were only the one, I'd be good,' then you might want to take a look at that.

"The funny thing is that I thought I could manage and get by once the drugs were out of the way. The keyword in that statement is 'thought.' My attitude was, what's next? I got this. If it were a drug problem, then the problem would be solved once I got rid of the drugs, right? Wrong. But the reality is that it's not a drug problem. Addiction is not going away that easily. The real underlying issues can't be solved with the same thinking that created them. I know this because I tried it. It's a personality problem with no cure; it only arrests when I apply changes to my thinking that roll down and affect my life, then further on into others' lives.

"Otherwise, if not arrested, it will increase and poison me and others. Filling myself with superficial things that only create more fantasies for me is not the outline I have come to know. I still have to pay bills, face consequences, work through feelings, and deal with life. For my program, I just need to get out of my way. My heart tells me to give myself a break. At the same time, more is being revealed daily.

"Today, I try not to put my key to happiness in someone else's pocket. I learned that lesson many times. Voids of the heart will go on; they hurt but always pass. But as I stick around, miracles grow; this is how I see recovery working in my life. I had a conversation one day with a friend about what they need in their life.

"Some words I remembered were 'I need to be *fixed.*' I do not believe that addiction can fix me. Nothing can permanently take me out of me and help me. In my experience, outside things only make me insane, obsessed, and compelled for one more."

As I finished talking, my mother smiled, and though the subject of addiction was still hard to understand, the words I said gave her the best tangible evidence of how addiction works for this addict.

She got up and looked at me, saying, "I will never ask you again, 'why can't you just quit?' It is starting to make sense now. Joey, it does all end the same, no matter what. It is just at different levels with different devils. Thank you."

I hugged my mother and left, knowing I had helped her connect with me and let her into my heart.

Chapter 3

QUIT CHOOSING AND GET CHOSEN

Being able to connect with my mother and help her understand what addiction indeed *is* was priceless. But I couldn't choose when that moment happened. Those moments are chosen for me. As in all life-changing moments chosen for me, my purpose was built on moments just like that.

My struggles were a lesson and a blessing, becoming my story. Our friends in life become divine appointments, carrying us through barriers that we can't get through alone. Sometimes it's only a hug that we need to get by, and other times it is guidance from someone who has walked the path before us. Either way, hope is passed on to us, sometimes without us even knowing.

An example of that occurred on a Saturday evening when I was helping my wife put clothes into storage. While moving a bin, I noticed my old Club Serenity shirt, which I designed years ago, back in 2015. I held the shirt in my hand and sat down.

Looking at the shirt, I remembered all my experiences with Club Serenity. Those experiences were moments that were chosen for me.

I sat back in my chair and relaxed as I thought about how Club Serenity chose me. It was a time when my friend Mark St. Cyr and I volunteered for Club Serenity, a local recovery club without any funds, located in a run-down building in deplorable conditions. This was a time in which addicts were stigmatized to such a degree that many were lost, having no hope, no path, and no support.

At the time, it was only Mark and I who were active on the club's board, which did not have a clear mission but rather served as a local hangout recovery club providing space to rent for Twelve Steps meetings.

It was a beautiful, sunny day, and Mark and I were trying to find ways to locate funding to keep the club afloat financially. It was noon, and Mark and I had just left the local bank.

I got in my car and thought, "What will we do?" I sat there as sweat ran down my face, worried our facility might get shut down due to our bills piling up. As I wiped the sweat off my face, I looked at the sticker on my dashboard that read "Never give up." I chuckled at myself and looked up in the air as if to thank God and say, "Yeah, I know. I'm not going to give up. I can't." I was just about to back my car up when Mark tapped on the car window, signaling me to get out. I turned off the car and got out to talk to him. Mark looked at me and said, "Hey, Joey, the club needs your ambition."

I laughed and said, "Hey, I am just being me. I don't know how to run any other way."

Mark also chuckled and said, "I know; that is why we really need you."

At that moment, I thought to myself and said, "No one has ever told me they needed me. Well, not for anything good, at least."

Mark put his hand on my shoulder and looked me in the eye, saying, "Why don't you be our president?"

Once again, I looked at Mark, smiled, and said to myself, "Well, God, if this is where you're leading me, I guess I'll go." I didn't know at that moment why this task was being asked of me, for it wasn't me doing the choosing.

I was being chosen, and I could not conceptualize this duty of mine. It was a moment in my life that I will never forget. It was 12:07 p.m. on a Monday, and little did I know that it would be a decision that would determine the fate of many.

I think that throughout life, many people miss life's message because they are too busy looking for the mess. I knew to accept what was happening and try not to understand it.

I looked back at Mark, shook his hand, and said, "I'll do it." A lifelong friendship started that day, and I am truly forever grateful.

Right out of the gate, I kept running, wanting to make a difference, and I wasn't going to take no for an answer. The Mon Valley community needed support and a safe place for addicts to go that gave them stability, and I was called on to make this happen.

The Mon Valley area in southwestern Pennsylvania encompasses three counties: Washington, Westmoreland, and Fayette. Charleroi, where Club Serenity is located, used to be known as the "Magic City." The magic I understood was its excellent economy that used to have people traveling for miles to come to shop. Nowadays, addiction has become a terror in this area and has taken its toll on the region. The magic has been lost for so long, and I believed that one day the magic could be brought back.

To me, I was on a mission from God. Words from my best friend, Lee Roberts, rang true in my head: "Don't be nervous; get in service." I knew we needed to be a 501(c)(3) tax-exempt organization, though I did not have any legal experience to make this happen.

All I had was faith, and that had to be enough. If I could keep going and, no matter what, not give up, I could figure it out eventually. My solution was easy: I would teach myself how to do it, somehow. I laughed.

I started watching YouTube videos to learn everything I could that would teach me how to be a paralegal basically. I then raised money for the filing fees and wrote all the necessary paperwork to file for the tax-exempt status. I ended up getting approved on the first try. The only thing I felt I did right was to not give up, and that was enough.

I remember in early recovery being told, "Recovery is 10 percent application and 90 percent showing up." I took those words to heart and ran with them, and it paid off.

From then on, if I needed help, I found it, and if I couldn't find help, I would do whatever it took to get it done. Mark knew he had the right person for the job, but I didn't stop there. The southwestern Pennsylvania Mon Valley community was suffering, and someone had to take a stand. I knew that someone had to be me. I just wanted to help, and service was exactly what the job required. Along the way, we faced society's dogma against addicts, which I didn't care for. I was up against a wall but knew that the wall would eventually crumble if I banged on it long enough.

Housing was a huge issue in our community, and Mark and I would have talks in the early days about creating recovery houses, but this was only a dream.

Though, once again, I remember being told, "Joey, don't forget, the people who get the freedom are those who do the work." I was willing to do the work, whatever it took, and I wasn't going to stop, no matter the cost. I felt that everyone was coming along for the ride on this recovery journey. I needed to find ways to help fill in the gaps with the community's disparities.

With housing in mind, I wrote a business plan for the first recovery house in the Mon Valley, along with the club's bylaws and other legal paperwork we were required to have. We were becoming a legitimate nonprofit business and organization, making dreams come true.

With the stigma growing in our community, the addicts looked to a recovery cowboy to stand up and advocate for change. As time progressed, some critical members joined our executive board, which focused on making a difference in our area. These new members, vital to the stability of our cause, were Mindi McCloy, Lee Roberts, and my future wife, Jodie Pagano.

These three people became my family, and we all played our part. We were a motley crew of individuals with great dedication to the cause. I wouldn't trade anything for them. They had the same passion that I had and knew that we could not and would not stop until the town heard our cry. Mindi, Lee, Jodie, and Mark were divine appointments who were all in this together and were placed in my life at the right time.

Two years after I became Club Serenity's president, the officers and I knew that the town of Charleroi still had the stigma surrounding addicts, which kept so many people in the dark and left them to wither away. We all persevered through it and would not stop, no matter how many barriers we faced. We knew it was up to us to pave the way for addicts to recover in the Mon Valley.

In the summer of 2016, I talked with the club's vice president, Lee Roberts, about how the community needed a recovery house. I said, "Lee, I will attend the next council meeting and speak about the club's needs."

Lee looked at me and said, "We need to continue to make a stand, and I think you're right, Joey. I feel that they will listen to you. I just don't know what to do. We have to do something, and Joey, you just might be the something they need."

I hugged him, walked out, sat in my car, and prayed. I put my arms around the steering wheel while resting my head on it, trying to reflect on the task at hand. I spoke out loud, saying, "God, why are you asking me to do this? I guess I just need to show up and you will do the rest." I was very ambiguous about the direction to go with the club, but I felt the decision to go to the council meeting and speak was in my heart.

Ten days later, I walked into my first council meeting in Charleroi, Pennsylvania. I knew I had to make an impact and set the tone for us. Town members had caught wind of us coming to the meeting, so it was a packed house.

About thirty minutes in, the meeting was silent, and the council president looked up at our group and said, "Mr. Pagano, what do you have to say concerning the club's matters?"

They handed me the microphone, and all eyes were on me. My mouth wouldn't open, but my heart spoke up. "We need the town's support, and we are not leaving until we get it. Addicts need housing and we are trying to build a recovery house in our community. The stigma in this community is killing addicts every day!"

Some council members seemed taken aback by my words, but others were compassionate toward our cause. Either way, Club Serenity was here to stay, and I was getting started making our mark in the community.

I attended several more council meetings and spoke to make a difference in our community. The town was starting to understand that we weren't going to leave, and the stigma was starting to crumble away.

As it kept receding, we started to see more hope in our community. It was around when I had been clean for three years and was still serving as president of the club.

Recovery flowed through my body as if I were on fire and needed to keep going with my life on the line. This was a period of steadily increasing overdoses happening at an alarming rate; the opioid epidemic was showing us that it was here to stay. It's comfortable to live by default with addiction and easy to settle. My disease put limits on me and let me decide quite often, as it cosigned my every move.

At Club Serenity, my role was simple: I continued to serve my community by being this "recovery cowboy." I just wanted to make a difference, and I did this by helping people get into treatment, fostering peer support, and being an advocate for them. I turned my car into the "recovery mobile" and had it wrapped with Club Serenity decals while it was in service. I was an unpaid volunteer and merely survived. Everything I had in my life directly resulted from helping someone else.

After four years of serving the community, I felt I was being led in a different direction, for Club Serenity was now a functioning entity, and more was being revealed about my story.

In my life, when my perspective changes, my season does as well. To me, seasons are not just like summer or winter, but rather times in my life when my purpose develops and shifts. I felt pulled into a new season built on the club's backbone.

Like the stigma in our community, the opioid epidemic had killed addicts by the thousands. It was a time when Governor Tom Wolf created the Centers of Excellence (COE) for opiate use disorder (OUD). PA.gov (2018) states, "Centers of Excellence have proven themselves to be a critical part of our efforts to improve treatment for people suffering from opioid use disorder." This was a pivotal time in the history of human services in Mon Valley and southwestern Pennsylvania.

While I served as the club's president, we attended outreach events all over to try to collaborate with agencies for support. One such time, we met with Southwestern Pennsylvania Human Services (SPHS) to see what financial support we could get to open a recovery house. Lee and I met with their staff, which included the chief operating officer (COO) at the time, Kellie McKevitt.

I remember meeting Kellie, for she was a human service soldier. I did not realize at first that I was in the presence of greatness. She shook my hand and looked into my eyes, seeing things in me that I did not yet see in myself. She was a legend, and, to me, legends never die. As COO of SPHS at the time, she played a critical part in the creation of the Centers of Excellence at SPHS. She understood that the Mon Valley, a region in southwestern Pennsylvania, desperately needed an assertive drug and alcohol team, and she needed this to come to fruition. Though it was not our time to join forces, much work still needed to be done. Our paths would soon cross again, as our destiny was intertwined.

Time passed as I grew in recovery, and I was pushed into the direction of SPHS. After meeting Kellie McKevitt at our meeting, I knew I needed to be of service in a different capacity, but I didn't yet know how.

One day I had a scheduled appointment with staff from SPHS, and I was still determining the exact reason for this meeting. I was told it was a discussion about the club's outreach and how we could get support from their agency.

In life, there are some days you can remember, like birthdays, holidays, and other essential family days. March 30, 2017, was more than one of those days; it was a day my life would be changed forever. This day is always in my heart; it is as if it is part of it, actually. I can always go back to it, for it has become part of me, just as if it happened yesterday.

While I rose from the bed, I looked at my alarm, which read 9:00 a.m. I yelled, "I need to get to the club quickly! I have to meet those two women from SPHS." As I looked out my bedroom window, I noticed the wind blowing outside, and I hoped this upcoming meeting went quickly. Later that day, I had to talk to someone who wanted opioid detox treatment, and the SPHS meeting needed to be brief. I got dressed, ran downstairs, and got ready to leave.

As my feet hit the pavement, I ran to the club, walked into my office, and sat down with a few minutes to spare. I glanced at the wall and read the sign, "Relax." I chuckled to myself with a grin that I could not put away. I looked at the clock and knew it was time for the appointment with Rita and Cheryld, whom I did not know.

The club's door opened while light glimmered on the hardwood floor. The two women dressed in matching purple outfits walked in, smiling, which was contagious, and their presence intrigued me. To me, they were like angels, the way they glowed as they walked in, which took me aback. As I shook their hands, a chill ran down my spine, and I couldn't at that moment figure out the cause.

I feel that sometimes in life, we are put in positions where we must make decisions that will affect the rest of our life. This was just that day. Little did I know that my purpose would soon be born from a conversation. COE supervisor Rita Nichols and Executive Director Cheryld Emala at the time walked in to convince me to work for them at SPHS. I did not have any plans to work for or even apply to SPHS, for my destiny, I thought, was to stay in Charleroi and live life by default as a recovery cowboy.

Both of them chimed in, looking me directly in the eyes, and said, "Joey, why don't you work for us and let us pay you. You can work at the COE and make a difference saving lives."

While echoing in my soul, those words pierced my heart and exploded without my permission. Rita and Cheryld were unexpected divine appointments. They were two innovators in a drug and alcohol program where staff would not give up on persons who sought treatment. As they talked, I smiled and felt their words. Little did I know that Kellie, Cheryld, and Rita would become family and help me develop into the person I am today. I could not conceptualize this yet, for I was still unsure where I fit. The stigma of addiction goes deep and affects us in our present. Times like this are when yesterday calls today and wants to be tomorrow.

As they left, I kneeled in prayer and yelled in my office, "I can't get paid; it just would not feel right. I don't know what to do!" My gut was in a knot, and the ambiguity was all over my face.

The thing about hope is that sometimes when words are spoken from someone's heart, they pierce a heart. That heart was mine, and the piercing was done without my permission. I got up, glanced at the wall at the end of the room in Club Serenity, and saw the sign "Expect a Miracle." "Wait, what miracle." I laughed as I said that, not knowing what was happening at that very moment; my life was about to change.

I did not expect the miracle that I found as I started my professional journey. As I agreed to work for SPHS, the day I was to start was upon me. It was 8:00 a.m., and I got out of my car and slowly walked toward the building. I paused to raise my head to look at the agency's iconic symbol. I was still unsure how I would fit into the COE. This is an agency where I was a client long ago when I could not find hope.

As I wiped the tears from my eyes, I realized I was part of something bigger than me. This moment was built on sacrifice and perseverance through life's storms and continuing to recover because there are no free rides in life—none! After all my scars, bruises, pain, and more *pain*, I had reached a point where most would have given in, but instead I kept going.

Addiction is a disease that ends many lives, takes everything in its path, and leaves nothing to spare. I made it through; yes, I'm doing it. I smiled, walked in, and let my purpose guide me.

As months passed at the COE, I started working with the medical director of SPHS, Scott A. Cook. Our relationship was built from the collaboration needed to better serve our populations in medically underserved areas (MUAs). In recovery medicine, meeting a client where the client is, rather than where the practitioner is, is a core principle.

Sometimes when you meet people in your life, they help keep you connected to your purpose and take you further than you can go alone. Dr. Cook was that person, and our shared beliefs would complement values like self-determination, empathy, and compassion, which are vital to serving our clients. As this relationship grew, it indeed embodied the shared attitude of "no addict left behind."

The memories I had from Club Serenity and the Centers of Excellence were part of me and led me to my purpose. After reflecting on all of this, I got up from my chair and said to myself, "What a long, strange trip it has been." I then looked at my wife and said, "Dear, I am so grateful to have been part of the club and the COE." She looked at me, smiled, and said, "Me too." Those memories helped to refine me into who I am today. And I thank God every day for the good and the bad, for those memories also made me who I am. These memories were of my path, for today is a gift built from yesterday's history.

Chapter 4

NOT ONLY A BROTHER BUT A BEST FRIEND

Though yesterday's history often comes with distress, sometimes blessings are hidden in the pain. We find that the struggle is the gift that makes us who we are today. The journey prepares us for what is to come. The tale of my brother, Xavier, who chose our family and taught us how to love again while missing my son, is a struggle that has become a blessing.

My son, Zavier, who is eighteen, and my brother, Xavier, who is eleven, are two people in my life whose stories are intertwined with moments that are kept locked in my heart. As bad as addiction ravaged my life, it still brought forth good and bad times that would change my life forever.

There were times when the thought of me not being able to see my son paralyzed my spirit. I would question myself at night, saying, "I want to be a dad so bad, but I do not know how. How can I explain to my son that I was sick, so sick, and addiction had me as its prisoner. It called the shots and it controlled my every move. I am so lost, and I wish I could just find my way out." I would go to sleep at night and pray that God would give me a sign or just shine a light in the darkness I lived in, and maybe, just maybe, I could escape this way of thinking. The funny thing is that God did not give me a sign; instead, he gave me a brother who would take my hand and show me the way out to my son's heart.

It still overwhelms me to look back at all the times that I did not do the choosing; instead, I was chosen by someone or something. While being chosen, I also learned that the greatest gifts in life come wrapped in strange packages. My brother, Xavier, was an example of one of my greatest gifts. He helped teach me many things that shaped me into the man I am today. My brother was another divine appointment who helped me get through a tough time in my life; without him, I would not have been able to. Addiction took my son away from me, and I felt lost without any hope. I wanted to be a dad but did not know how. Sometimes it is funny how God works, I think. This was another moment when good things had to end for wonderful things to begin.

I often think of this story, but it still amazes me how it happened. It was something that I did not see coming, though it changed our lives forever. One day I was driving with my brother, and he asked how he came to our family. I told him the narrative so he could understand.

I told him, "Xavier, you came to our family through some hard-won experiences." I was struggling with active addiction, and it was not a fun place for an addict. It was a time when I begged

God to let me die so that the madness could stop. I was living to use and using to live, and I didn't know where to turn. It was a day I lived by default; whatever happened that day was my reality. I would do anything to take me out of myself, and this day it would be sexual relations with a woman I barely knew.

If there was a way for me to leave this world, I needed to find it fast; instead, I was slowly dying by suicide. I was in an apartment with a lady as she fell asleep. I knew I needed to leave, so I put on my hoodie while walking toward the door, still dope sick and wanting to die. I tried to close the door quietly as I walked out of the apartment. After I left, I looked at the ground while grabbing my legs, almost falling since I was so tired. I knew I needed to go far away to a place where I could be alone and no one could find me, for I was very sick and hoping to pass out.

I yelled out, "Please, God, just let me die and leave this miserable existence! I have had enough of this pain!" As those words came out of my mouth, I realized I might wake up the tenant in the nearby house, so I ran as fast as possible until I was blocks away. As I ran, tears streamed down my face and would not stop.

Sadly, these tears would continue for months until I eventually turned myself in to the police and hoped for a new beginning. Almost a year later, I would be sitting in a prison cell, hoping to die, with no hope in sight, crying myself to sleep. On this day, I was woken up to take a paternity test for a child, and I did not recognize his name on the document. After taking the test, I was told the result would not be in for several months. During this time, I called my family, asking them to track down this child's whereabouts and see if this was real. My family found Xavier's mother and called her to try to facilitate a meeting between them to see what this was all about. His biological mother's name was Ashley, and she was also in recovery from addiction, like me.

The next section is told from my father's perspective (Tim), so as to give the best account of this story.

My wife, Cindy, and I were at my daughter Samantha's house. I was nervous about meeting this child, for there was a chance he could be my grandson. I was pacing around the house, waiting for Ashley to bring him over.

I just wanted to be called "Pap" one time! I missed Joe's son so much! This was something that would be priceless to me. I had so much sadness in my heart from not seeing my grandson, Zavier, that this might be my last chance to be a grandfather. My son's addiction hurt our family, and maybe, just maybe, this child could put my heart back together again. Though I wasn't sure if there was any chance that we might be whole again.

As I continued to pace, I heard a knock on the door, and the room went quiet. It had to be Ashley bringing Xavier.

We all stared at the door as Samantha yelled, "Come in!"

My breathing slowed as she walked into the house with Xavier in her arms. I thought, "I think he looks like Joe." She sat down on the chair and Xavier stared at me, as if he could look right through my soul. His blue eyes were so big, and I could tell he was intrigued by me, as his eyes would not leave my face.

"Ashley, can I hold him?" I asked.

She replied, "Of course." As I reached for him, he reached back to me and it felt as if love pierced my heart without my permission. I would have never chosen this situation, although Xavier was choosing me. My wife and daughter smiled as I held him, knowing that this child was right where he belonged. I couldn't explain what happened that day, but it was something I would have never expected to happen that day.

This was the day we all will never forget, for it was the day Xavier changed our lives, and even through all of the dark times that addiction brought, it was a six-month-old child who had the power to put our hearts back together again.

The next part of this story is from my perspective. In the spring, I was released from prison and moved in with my family. This same day, the paternity test results returned and showed that I was not the father of Xavier. While he got older, Ashley would continue to struggle with addiction, each time getting worse and worse. Even with her addiction and my not being the father, my family did not care; they had fallen in love with this child and were going to do whatever they could to save him.

Since Ashley's addiction would not stop, my parents stepped up and became foster parents, and now they were the primary caregivers for the child. Xavier and I bonded as I was learning to care for him while still missing my son, Zavier. He might not have been my son, but he became part of me, and I also fell in love with him.

Time progressed; Xavier was four years old and Ashley still

struggled with addiction. My parents then adopted him after Ashley's parental rights were terminated.

I remember my father saying, "We will not let anything happen to this child. I love him and we are going to fight for him." The adoption process was a hard one, as we were challenged by Ashley's mother. We would not give up or back down. We were all that Xavier had, and we would continue to love him, no matter what the cost.

Once again, a miracle happened as our family was granted the adoption, and I now had a brother. Once again, I did not choose this moment, for it chose us. Amid all the horrors that addiction created for us, Xavier was the hope that brought us back together. I did not realize what had happened then, but the miracle of Xavier's life gave me hope.

As the years passed, Xavier and I became best friends, and although I still missed my son, I did not have the courage to see him. Addiction shamed me, and I felt inadequate as a father. My brother was one of the best things to ever happen to me and was the divine appointment who chose me.

This part is told from Xavier's perspective.

My brother Joey and I were in his room playing video games, which was my favorite thing to do. Joey was depressed and missing his son, and I could tell he was sad. I asked him, "Joey, what's wrong, bro?"

He looked at me with a tear in his eye, replying, "I hope to one day see my son again, Xavier."

I hugged him and said, "Listen, Joey, one day, he's going to see what I see in you. You are the best brother, and I appreciate it every day. I don't know what I would do without you. You, mom, and dad saved me, and I know if anything ever goes wrong, you'll be there for me. Thank you, Joey."

Joey nodded his head and said, "Thank you, Xavier."

The next section is back to my perspective.

From then on, I knew that it wasn't me taking care of him, but him taking care of me. He said the words I needed to hear when times were rough. Sometimes all a person needs is a hug, which makes all the difference. Xavier was not only my brother but my best friend, and I wouldn't trade him for the world.

Chapter 5

GET BUSY LIVING OR GET BUSY DYING

We must never give up on our families, even through our darkest times. Xavier became my best friend, and he learned how important it is not to leave me behind. It was time to get busy living and be that example of a beacon of light to him just as he was to me. Though, there was a time when I was busy dying one day at a time. In these moments, hope can be found with just a shimmer of light as long as I open my eyes.

* * *

This memory is in my heart, and I will never let it go. It keeps me in recovery and reminds me of where I came from. It has hurt and helped me. It helped one day when I was driving through my hometown. It was 9:00 a.m., and I drove past the police station and saw a homeless lady sitting on the curb across the street. Her clothes were disheveled, and she had a sad look on her face. It was a look that I remembered all too well. It was as if I could feel her emotions just by looking at her.

As I pulled over toward her, a chill went down my spine. I rolled down my window and stared at her eyes, though she would not look up at me. I said, "Ma'am, are you okay?" She would not answer me but continued to stare at the ground while resting her hands on her chin. "Ma'am, ma'am, are you?"

She looked at me before I could get all of the words out of my mouth. She still had her sad look but was staring at me, waiting for me to speak again. I left the car instead and walked toward her, but she didn't take her eyes off me. Once I got to the woman, I sat down next to her. As we sat close to each other, it appeared time had come to a standstill. At that moment, it seemed that we were the only people on the street.

There weren't any sounds when I started to speak. "Are you okay?" I asked, trying to engage her.

She finally replied, "I am. I am just tired. I got into an argument with my ex-boyfriend and felt like I was at my breaking point."

I started to smile, saying, "I feel you. I saw you sitting here and was worried if you were okay, and I just wanted to make sure there wasn't anything I could do. I know this curb, for it still holds memories in my heart, ma'am."

Her eyes widened as if she was even more intrigued by my story and hoped I would continue to expand on that thought. Even though I did not know this lady, I felt compelled to tell her my story, for we had a connection now and I knew those words from my heart would touch her heart.

I looked at her and said, "Let me take you back to the time when I almost didn't come back."

This story might be yesterday's history, but it is part of who I am. I then started telling her my story. "It was years ago and I was stuck in addiction. A lost soul, searching for something, but I didn't know what."

"If I could just get some sleep!" I muttered to myself, trying to keep my eyes closed, praying for rest. But with my eyes open, I stared at the clock, watching the seconds pass. I couldn't go on like this, and I knew it. I tried to stand up from lying on the couch, but the fever, chills, and muscle aches kept me paralyzed while sweat dripped off my face.

As I raised my head, the disease of addiction whispered in my ear, "You need to get up and find something to get you off sick, Joey." I just wanted this madness to end and prayed to God it would.

The sun was coming up, and I knew I had to leave or the dope sickness would continue to paralyze me. I put on my hoodie as I walked out the door, ready to do whatever I had to do to be well. As I walked down the street, the disease of addiction was holding a meeting in my head. "Joey, keep marching, and I will take care of you."

I tried shutting these thoughts off, but at that moment, I felt hopeless. I had no way financially to get my fix and knew that if I did not keep marching, death was the only other path. I could not bear another day of this dope sickness; maybe I could somehow overdose, and it would all end. Perhaps someone could put me out of my misery.

My disease was yelling at me in my mind, saying, "Let's go! I don't care how tired you are. You're going to march until you get your fix, Joey."

The dope sickness had me sweating profusely. I could barely feel my legs, but they kept moving as if I were back in the army, taking orders from my sergeant. I had no control of my mind at this time, for it was hijacked by my addiction. As I marched through town, I saw a gas station up ahead, which I knew might have what I needed to get my fix.

A tiny part of me fought my addiction and argued in my mind while my disease ensured it was in control. "Joey, you need to get high now! Don't wait another minute! You'll stay sick, and you don't want to do that, do you?"

I was now conversing with myself as I stood on the sidewalk across from the store. Cars that drove past were staring at me, wondering what was wrong with me. I yelled back to my addiction, "God, please help me! I'm not strong enough; just kill me, please." I knew my disease was winning and calling the shots as I marched across the street.

While approaching the gas station, I kneeled and looked at the sky, pleading, "God, just take me out of this world and end this madness, please!"

The disease answered me and said, "Joey, you are going to march in there and get some cash. Now, go!"

I walked into the store as if some outside force had pulled me. Sweat and tears were rolling down my face, and I still had fever chills from the dope sickness. Now in the store, I pulled my hood over my head, ashamed of myself and believing the worker would not recognize me. I tried to pray while my addiction was pulling my strings as if I were a puppet. I said to myself, "Maybe they will shoot and kill me and this madness will be over. Yes, just maybe."

I then robbed the register and ran out as quickly as I could. I kept running until I could find somewhere to get my fix.

I was so tired, but my disease said, "Keep going and don't stop until you get what *we* need, Joey. Remember, you *need* me, Joey." I was blacking out and couldn't think straight as I ran until I got my fix and then found myself at the park alone, trying to get high.

Sitting down, I yelled, "God, can you please just take me and let this all end! I can't do this anymore! Let me overdose again! I'm by myself; no one can revive me; I am ready to go. Take me! Take me, please!" My thoughts would not stop racing as I was about to use the last of my drugs. My heart was now speaking to me, which told me to leave and walk to town.

I decided to start walking and then hitchhiked to town. I stopped one block from the police station, sat down on the curb, and called my mother. She answered the phone, sounding frantic, asking me if I was okay. I told her, "Mom, I am either turning myself in to the police or I am going to kill myself. I can't take this madness anymore. I just want to die! If I had a gun, I would just end my life now. My head won't turn off." I thought to myself, I don't know what to do.

She yelled, "What did you do?"

I muttered back to her, "I can't stop using—this is going to be the last time you will talk to me," and then hung up the phone. As I hung up, my mother screamed while she cried. I kneeled and prayed, "God, please help and give me the strength to go on."

My history with the police was not good, but I knew that I had to find someone to trust, for I couldn't trust myself. I did not know at this time, but the officers would become divine appointments who answered my prayers without me even knowing. I did not have any strength to get up, but at this time, it was as if I was being carried across the street with a power not of my own.

I opened the door to the police station and walked through it, telling the officer, "Please arrest me, for I was the one who robbed the store. I can't stop using drugs; if I don't stop, I will die."

They took me into custody immediately, and a calm feeling came over my body. I knew it was over, and I could finally rest. To me, this all happened the day before I would die. This surrender was a gift, for it let me live in the here and now. It will always be my history, though it will not define who I am. This dark moment was a lesson and a blessing I will forever hold close to my heart.

I can never repay my gratitude to the police, who never gave up on me, even in my darkest times. Arresting me was the best thing that ever happened to my addiction. In my heart, I believe that I walked into the station the day before I would die.

As I finished telling my story, the lady looked at me, grabbed my hand, and said, "Thank you. You shared your history with me, and I am grateful. Your story has shown me how sometimes things happen for you rather than to you. It is as if I can look at my situation differently. I appreciate you, sir."

I nodded and said, "No problem. I feel we were meant to meet, ma'am. I hope everything is okay with your relationship, but if it is not, I will pray for you."

The lady stood up, looked at me for the last time, and put her hand on her heart before leaving.

I got back in my car and sat there for a while. I let out a big breath, looked up, and said, "Thank you, God, for everything, the good and the bad. Yesterday's history is truly a gift."

Chapter 6

YESTERDAY'S HISTORY, TOMORROW'S A MYSTERY, AND TODAY'S A GIFT

Getting busy living helped me gain stability through life's storms. There will always be struggles that we have to persevere through. Sometimes it will be our history, and other times, a mystery. To me, the true secret of life is being able to appreciate the present, which is our gift.

I came to realize that growing up in recovery was a challenging task. I could not figure out how to process emotions that had been stuck in time for decades. How do you stay in the moment in a world constantly on the go? Who wants to wait for anything? Recovery takes time, just as it took addiction a lifetime to change my thinking. Thank God for yesterday's history; better believe tomorrow is a mystery. What's blessed is that today is a gift. My past has already been written, so why dwell on it? I *do not live there today*, for my future is uncertain, so why project? Why? Why are *these words* so hard to swallow and believe? These thoughts I reflected on, for recovery isn't easy, no matter how long I have been clean.

Remaining stuck in those memories kept me sick and lost. The memories would be like pop-ups that couldn't stay popped. I would remember one and then raise my head and yell, "If I could just get these thoughts out of my head!"

My mind continued to race and speak to me, saying, "Joey, you know that the pain and suffering are only waiting down that street!" It is only the here and now that *truly* belongs to me. I would wonder if I was the only one this happened to. Could anyone relate? Because it is horrible to be trapped in a never-ending nightmare of the past that I can't escape, and, well, it just keeps playing on repeat! *Will it ever end?*

"Joey, do not forget about your hell!" To me, it is so much more than a place you can go! It is that mental repeat cycle! It's my mind getting hijacked due to not dealing with me. That good ole fear of the unknown, isn't that a lovely thing? I'll sometimes be afraid of fear! Not anything, fear itself. Those "shoulda, coulda, woulda" thoughts keep me in a never-ending attraction to my past that can't be changed, forgotten, edited, or erased; it can only be accepted. Trying to stay clean was not an easy task, though I felt I was spared and had a purpose today, and that was why I kept going.

Speaking of purpose, I can remember moments that provided me with evidence that I was still on the right track. One day, I was working with a client in my office when she looked at my diplomas on the wall.

She asked me, "How did you attain these? I can only dream of doing that. I am an addict, and I just don't think it is possible for me."

I replied, "I am also an addict." At that moment, she understood and was given hope. It was that principle that someone could pass on to another.

She left my office, and I sat down to relax. I looked at the wall and remembered the day those dreams came true.

I was standing in the convocation center at my university. I looked to my left and saw my family smiling as I walked in line to graduate with my master of social work. A chill ran down my spine as I closed my eyes and quietly said, "Thank you, God, for why I was spared. Why is it me that gets to walk?"

A tear ran down my face as a fellow student hugged me and said, "We did it!" Those words pierced my heart like getting hit by lightning.

Just then, it was as if my question was being answered, just in a different way. I asked such a question because sometimes I feel that I did not do anything special to get here. It didn't have to be this way, I thought. I didn't understand why the other friends I used to have didn't make it. I remember conversing with a lost soul who passed on due to an overdose. We had two years clean and were celebrating together. I thought they would go on to college instead of me, for it was their dream too, just like mine. It was hard to stay in the moment and not focus on the past. My past was filled with me giving up on everything—EVERYTHING! I believed that it was not worth trying if I had the slightest chance of failing.

My past was all the evidence I needed to fuel that belief system. Little did I know that the friend I thought would go to college, not me, would soon take their last breath.

As I walked toward the stage to receive my diploma, I smiled and accepted it instead of trying to understand why it was just me there. I stepped forward, shaking the dean's hand as I grabbed my diploma.

I then approached my wife, who hugged me and said, "I am so proud of you!" This was the girl who stole my heart and had me at hello.

I smiled and realized that our past does not dictate our future. Tomorrow is a mystery, with so much that is unwritten.

I stood up from my chair, grabbed my coat, turned out the lights, and got ready to leave my office. I glanced at my diplomas as I walked out the door, again feeling a sense of gratitude, once again realizing how precious today's gift is.

The next day, I took in a new document to hang up on my wall at work. This item complemented my diplomas and made my job possible. The journey of attaining this document was the longest journey of my life. I can remember each moment leading up to the day I had it granted. Just as I hung it up, a client came into the office and said, "Joey, I also want to be a licensed social worker but have criminal charges and don't know what to do. Please tell me what you did."

I looked back at her, smiled, and said, "It took a lot of work and perseverance. I remember the last days of this process as if it happened yesterday." I started telling her the story, as her eyes opened wide.

✳ ✳ ✳

I was in my governor's pardon hearing via Zoom video conference. I was so nervous as I looked at the screen; it was my turn to be assessed.

The lieutenant governor, John Fetterman, asked me, "Do you have anything to say, sir?"

I looked up and said, "Governor, I am sorry for my crimes, for I am in recovery now and doing what I can to serve. I believe I must never give up hope and I will continue to do what I can for others who share the same pain. Sir, everything I have in my life directly results from helping someone else. I am just grateful to be here."

My heart was beating fast as I paid attention to every word the lieutenant governor said. The politicians were all looking at me as I held my head up high, having faith in my actions and knowing I was exactly where I was supposed to be.

This was a time in my life when I could remember the exact moment that fueled my purpose. It was a time when God put his hand on my shoulder and told me to keep going. Grace is an unmerited favor. It was something that I was given that day.

I stayed in position and knew that I was in the care of God. It was a feeling that overtook me and assured me that everything would be fine, no matter what. Whatever happened that day, I knew I needed to persevere and continue my journey.

After I was done talking, John Fetterman looked at me and told my lawyer that he didn't need to hear anything more from her. I knew then that it would be okay, whatever decision was made. The Board of Pardons voted to approve my pardon that day, and a tear ran down my face. I knew then that the people who get freedom are the people who do the work. I did the work, continued to show up to serve, and bet my life on that.

Months later, Governor Tom Wolf signed my pardon, which was a lost dream that God saw me through once again. I knew that I could use this experience to help others and become a vision of hope for them. This addict would not be left behind, for today was a gift.

* * *

The client thanked me for my story, realizing that it was possible for her to do this. I replied, "Listen, all I did was show up for life, not back down when life's struggles knocked me back. Yesterday does contain my history, but tomorrow's mystery is worth fighting for. I must never give up, for if I do, I will miss the gift, which is today. Believe me, you can do it too."

For anyone in recovery, they become a vision of hope, and their light can shine so bright that people from all over the world can be changed by their glow. One such girl became a light for me, and it took most of my life to see it. I always wanted everything to happen today, but "today" is such a powerful word for an addict. For some people, it never comes and they will always live in yesterday. I remember one of those yesterdays when I was ready to give up on dating. This was a day when I needed help conceptualizing what a healthy relationship looked like.

If I had kept that mindset, I would have remained in those endless tomorrows.

The truth is that behind every great man is a great woman, and behind every great woman is a great man. Today, the journey to a healthy relationship is a broken road full of memories, good and bad. These memories have been tattooed on me with ink that will forever remind me of the journey.

The journey, captured on my right-arm tattoo sleeve, tells the story of my life. This story was built by hard-won experiences that shaped me. I am now married, but it almost never happened. I could not let go of yesterday's history and could not wait for the mystery that tomorrow held either. I had to learn through experience what the gift was. And that gift was a relationship built on communication, compromise, and commitment to hard work.

Being in a toxic relationship at a crossroads kept me stuck in a place where I found distorted comfort, which gave me some familiar pain. I am the type of person who desires love but would quickly settle for sex. In my life, relationships would often come and go. Jodie was one of my best friends in recovery and always seemed to be by my side. I remember the first day I met her; we were at a recovery meeting, and she was trying to stay clean. She was excited about recovery, just as I was, and she was a vision of hope to many. She didn't know that yet.

I was reading a book when Jodie first came up to me, saying, "What's up?"

I sat there dumbfounded, not knowing who she was. Her face

was red. I could tell she was nervous about speaking, but she was doing it anyway.

Jodie smiled. "Joey, get up, get...up. I want to hug you. I'm new and want to meet everyone here."

She reached down, pulled me up, put her arms around me, and gripped me tightly. It was as if I could feel her excitement in that hug. There is a lot to say about a new person in recovery. The passion they have is indescribable.

I could still feel her as I sat down after we broke away from that hug. We stayed clean, kept running in recovery, and became best friends.

I then was single again and wasn't feeling well, so I turned to my friends for support. Sometimes the most unexpected things happen at the most unexpected times. This was a time just like that. As with other decisions in my life, it worked out when I quit choosing and was chosen. I did not have a plan to date Jodie; our mutual friend pointed out how it might be a good idea to date, and I didn't see it the whole time.

Jodie was my best friend, and I decided to take a leap of faith with her, which paid off. We have been together since that day. We got married on September 3, 2018, and I was about to give up on a decision before it even happened. If I had done that, I would have never known the love I have today.

If you asked me to describe what love is in our relationship, I would do it this way. Some believe that "those who matter don't judge, and those who judge don't matter." I'm afraid I have to disagree with that statement. Jodie and I judge each other in our relationship and know every flaw we have and don't have. Love is about not giving up on each other, no matter the cost. If you can love the person you are with after knowing their flaws and judging them, then that is true love. That is what we have.

In a relationship, yesterday will always have some history, and your tomorrow might still be a mystery, but never let go of today because it will always be a gift that lives on forever. Jodie and I won't leave each other behind. No matter what.

Chapter 7

A-Z ABSTINENCE TO MAT

Today's gifts are so powerful that they can change the course of your life and guide you off the beaten path. There was a time when I was so caught up in how I needed to recover that I remained stuck and never experienced recovery for myself. I always thought that you needed to recover how everyone else recovered. Recovery is as broad as A–Z, abstinence to MAT. I had to not forget that autonomy was my compass, as Jodie reminded me when we discussed our recovery. With both of us in recovery and working in the field, this subject has come up a lot in our talks.

One day my wife and I got home from work and were both tired, trying to relax, but we started to discuss our recovery. Not only is my wife in recovery, but she utilized medication-assisted treatment (MAT) before getting clean. She currently advocates for people to choose their own path of recovery rather than it being forced on them.

As we talked, I looked at my wife and said, "Today at work, I spoke to Dr. Scott Cook about the importance of meeting a client where they were and not giving up on them no matter what."

She nodded and said she could empathize with me and see how important that is when genuinely trying to bridge the gap while working with clients in the drug and alcohol field.

I could hear the conviction in her words, not just because I was her husband, but also because as a recovery soldier she had had her own struggles and persevered through them.

Regarding MAT, Jodie has become a beacon of light for anyone seeking that treatment. It is crucial for a person seeking treatment to connect with someone who is not just a professional but also has life experience in that treatment modality.

As time progressed, I tried to relax while Jodie leaned toward me as if she was intrigued by my dialogue. We had a profound connection based on our recovery history and took our intimacy to new levels. We both got clean because "we hurt" and "we wanted" to get clean. We didn't get clean because someone said that "we have to" and "we needed to do it a specific way." In my experience, recovery only works with love and autonomy, not uniformity and governance. Jodie and I knew this all too well.

We continued to talk about this subject because it hit home. We sat down then, and I reflected on my past. I thought of a time when I felt I had to live by someone else's creed, and I wasn't doing it right unless I did. Words would ring out: "You'll never stay clean! You know there is only one way, Joey, and you're just going to die. You are just a lost cause! Why are you even trying?" My mind kept racing and would not stop, for my disease would not stop talking to me. It was a moment when the left side of my brain kept trying to sell me that idea, and the right side of my brain was trying to buy it. My mind would not shut off.

My addiction was giving orders, saying, "Hey, Joey, listen up. I know you can hear me! Maybe suicide would be a better way, Joey, just maybe." The stigma and creed of how I needed to work my recovery were buried deep in my thoughts and would not let go. It was as if I needed to get clean like others did, and my choice did not matter anymore.

I went to the window and pulled the shade down, which was a blanket. It was all I had left that I did not sell to the pawn shop. I laid back in my bed and curled up in the fetal position, trying not to believe what my mind told me.

I thought to myself, "If I can't just stay clean off everything, then was it even worth it to try? Was it?" Though my journey ended in an abstinence-based program, getting there was a hard road. We live in a world where uniformity and control rule the land regarding recovery medicine. Unity and autonomy take a back seat in a nation where the stigma keeps people suffering long after the expiration date.

There are many tools a person can choose to help them on their journey to stay clean of illicit substances. They range from abstinence-based twelve-step programs to counseling, therapy, mental health treatment, recovery houses, medication-assisted treatment, inpatient care, and detox. While working with Dr. Scott A. Cook in multiple behavioral health settings, clients have been assessed clinically to determine the best modality of care suited to their case. The COE of SPHS meets clients where they are, not where the care navigator (i.e., caseworker) is, to ensure that the client is agreeable to the care they are receiving. If a person seeking recovery is not ready, the practitioner can't say the right thing. However, if the person is ready, the practitioner can't say the wrong thing.

I then looked at my wife and, with strong conviction in my voice, said, "Jodie, I want you to understand where Dr. Cook and I came from in our talk. I know you share the same belief system as we do. We are trying to find a way to have other practitioners in our field continue to help clients, regardless of the level of care they need clinically, or they will agree to personally."

Looking through the lens of Dr. Scott A. Cook, a physician, requires a recovery medicine state of mind, and, most importantly, there is no addict left behind. I grabbed Jodie's hand and said to her, "I'll take you back to let you view his perspective through your eyes."

It was a day that Dr. Cook and I were at work discussing the different treatment modalities available to any person seeking recovery. I looked at him and said, "Dr. Cook, please expand on your thoughts on recovery medicine treatment. Help me better understand a perspective coming from a physician who has worked in this field for many years and helped thousands."

He said that for many practitioners in the field, there is a love-hate relationship with the word "addict." We love it because it is honest, real, descriptive, and without any sugarcoating. We hate the word because, from a provider standpoint, it seems derogatory and judgmental. There is a push in addiction medicine to change the name of the field to recovery medicine. This change highlights the eventual goal of getting people from the rough terrain of active addiction, across the bridge of hope, and onto the soft sand of recovery. It is certainly an attempt to destigmatize an area of medicine associated with much stigma.

It would surprise most patients and family members to know the derogatory terms used by healthcare providers and healers when discussing a patient suffering from substance use disorder. In private, when doctors and nurses collaborate about substance use patient care, the lack of compassion and stigma is often evident.

Healthcare providers are not immune to the stigma that permeates society regarding individuals addicted to substances. Outpatient treatment from A to Z includes abstinence to medication-assisted treatment (MAT). This spectrum of treatment options is fluid and dynamic as opposed to rigid and static. Many forms of outpatient engagement and treatment can positively impact a person suffering from a substance use disorder. Abstinence-based twelve-step programs like Alcoholics Anonymous (AA) and Narcotics Anonymous (NA) are on one end of the spectrum, and MAT is on the other end.

Additionally, patients might need to be admitted to a facility for more intense inpatient treatment when outpatient care fails. There are various levels of care between the extremes, and treatment should be individualized because there is no one-size-fits-all approach. The individual personality and circumstances of the patient must be considered. The various forms of treatment include the following:

- Abstinence-based twelve-step programs (AA and NA)
- Individual drug and alcohol therapy
- Mental health treatment
- Group therapy
- Drug and alcohol counseling
- Engagement with social work
- Sober living houses
- Outpatient medication-assisted treatment
- Intensive outpatient care
- Partial hospitalization
- Short-term inpatient residential rehabilitation
- Long-term inpatient residential rehabilitation
- Inpatient substance use detoxification

The different types of treatment are just like tools inside a toolbox.

Depending on the unique circumstance of the object needing to be fixed, one tool might work better as compared to another.

At times, a combination of tools is necessary to treat a patient. Keeping an open mind and being creative are what is essential, along with understanding that trial and error will be part of fixing anything broken and needing repair.

As we continued to talk, his words helped me understand a physician's perspective and why they think the way they do. We both worked in the field, and each had our own reasons for having so much compassion for someone trying to recover. We both knew that it was up to us to help a person get whatever tool they needed for their toolbox. We also always believed that self-determination is as important as our clinical and medical work.

Jodie's face got red, and I could tell that these words were close to her heart. From hearing Dr. Cook's words, she understood that although recovery pathways are A–Z, abstinence to MAT, there is no cookie-cutter process for anybody.

I could feel Jodie's pulse as I slowly let go of her hand while getting up to walk away.

As I turned my head toward my wife, she thanked me with a short response: "I love you, dear. Thank you for letting me into your mind."

I knew then that my wife and I had a connection that helped us grow as practitioners and partners.

Our connection was built from our personal struggles. Addiction is a family disease that Dr. Cook, Jodie, and I understood well. With this disease, when one person uses, the whole family suffers.

Chapter 8

ADDICTION IS A FAMILY DISEASE: ONE PERSON USES, BUT THE WHOLE FAMILY SUFFERS

As much as recovery is individualized, so is parenting. Being a mother to an addict is not an easy task. Much of this chapter is told by my mother, Cindy, whose experiences are individualized, just like the addict's. This is to let other parents transform into her role and know that even when your child is lost in addiction, there is hope.

✳ ✳ ✳

My name is Cindy Pagano, and I am a mother from Charleroi, a city close to Pittsburgh, Pennsylvania. I have a son who has struggled with addiction for decades. I was born in the baby boomer era when addiction was not yet looked at as a disease, and addicts were few and far between. In my generation, an addict was someone who was not looked at with any form of grace. Sadly, back then it was just easier to hide or deny a child's existence as an addict than to accept them for what they were. "All I ever wanted was for him to stay clean. I wanted him to have a better life than I had." Mothers often become collateral damage from a disease that takes no prisoners. I am a mother who had to learn how to love my son while not letting myself die in the process.

One day when I was working in the ICU at the local hospital and was leaving the floor to take my break, a lady approached me, asking if I could give her some of my time. I told her no problem, as I thought it was strange how the lady approached me. She looked very stressed, and her dark purple eyes looked straight through me.

I could see a tear falling from her eye as we sat down in the break room. I sat across from her, and now she grabbed my hand while crying a little more.

The lady turned to me and said, "Cindy, I don't know what to do! My son will not stop using! I feel that I am going to have to watch him die! Please help, please! I am having a mental breakdown and I don't know where to turn."

She put her head down as those words came out, still crying. I glanced at her and grabbed both of her hands, looking into her eyes and saying, "You can make it through this! I have faith in you. Don't give up, don't! You need to hold on, no matter what."

As I spoke to her, I could see her sad look turn into a smile, and these words pierced her heart. I went over to her and hugged her. I whispered in her ear, "Listen, I am not going to tell you what to do, but I can show you." Still hugging her, I knew I needed to tell her my story. I said, "Listen to my words as I tell you this, for I can feel your pain. I know that pain shared is pain lessened. Here is how it went."

✴ ✴ ✴

I remember those days as if it were yesterday. The sun was rising on an early Sunday morning; I slowly opened my eyes from another restless night of sleep. My head was pounding, forcing me to get up. I yelled, "Please, God, not another day of this. I just can't take it! What did I do to deserve this?" I tiptoed, coming to the room at the end of the hall; it was my son's room. The door was ajar, just as it had been the night before. I went to it, hoping not to hear anything. Slowly opening the door, my heart beat faster and faster while sweat rushed down my face. There wasn't anyone in the bed, which did not surprise me, though I still fought tears that I wasn't ready to let go of yet.

I fell to the floor and kneeled as I walked into the room. I then stared at a cross on his nightstand while slowly muttering the words, "Why do I have to endure this day after day? God, can you just take him this time?" My voice got louder as the words came out. "He does not need to suffer anymore." I picked up a coffee mug and threw it at the wall, shattering it to pieces. I yelled, "Take him! TAKE HIM!" Just then, another child came into the room, my daughter, Samantha, who was five years younger than Joey, collateral damage to the living hell we called home.

I yelled, "Get out of here, Samantha! Can't you see I'm praying." I could hear Sam talking quietly as she walked away. "I just wanted to hug my brother." Sadly, Joey was a prisoner too far gone and I was grieving my son, who was still alive.

I left the room and approached my husband, a man who did not recognize me anymore, for I was a shell of my former self. As we sat down on the couch, the door opened and my son walked in. He was wearing old, torn clothes, long sleeves and a coat in August weather. I ran to Joey and hugged him as he stood emotionless. My husband, Tim, could not get up and held his head in his hands in sadness. I pushed my son back and yelled, "Get out or go to treatment. I can't take it anymore; you are KILLING ME! KILLING US!"

As tears ran down Joey's face, he paused, breathed, and said, "I'll go after you give me some money. I need money. I must get some money! Please, Mom! Please. I'm fine, trust me! I am."

I yelled, "How can you be fine! We don't even see you anymore; you never eat and you keep losing weight!" This type of argument went on every night, every moment. It consumed our family's interactions.

While this was going on, Sam curled up in her bed, crying and hoping the yelling would stop. She told me she would silently whisper and pray, "Please, God, help my brother. Bring him back to me. I miss him."

At the same time, downstairs, I yelled, "Get out now! Do not ever come back! EVER! You're not my son anymore!"

As he walked out the front door, Sam quietly stepped down the stairs, trying to rush to see her brother one last time, to give him one last hug. But she was too slow to catch him and he was gone.

Sometimes I would say to myself, "Am I crazy to keep loving him?" I was the one person who loved Joey unconditionally, the person who gave him life and had his back no matter what. This experience taught me that sometimes the person we are the most supportive of is the one who is the most unsupportive of us. My son couldn't understand why I stayed the distance after all the manipulation, torment, and hell he put me through.

The day—the exact moment—I quit being afraid of what could go wrong and quit letting my son take control of my life, I was able to wake up, once and for all.

I started getting excited about all the things that could go right and started living.

"Why stay stuck in the problem for so long?" I would state. Most importantly, I would tell other parents who were suffering with children in addiction, "Throughout my life, I have encountered two types of pain, one that hurts me and one that changes me. I stayed stuck in unnecessary suffering time and time again and grew with the good experiences as well as bad ones."

As a parent, my message was clear: "See, if I don't like something about myself, I can change it now; I do not have to wait until the pain is unbearable." I would often say, "I can sit in some unbearable pain that most people would let go of much quicker."

One day, with a sigh of relief, I said, "Today, I must put myself first and foremost and work on self-love! I have learned that my greatest act of self-love is loving my son from a distance and saying no, no matter what the cost. Loving them from a safe place for me is a priority."

I would say, "There needs to be a line drawn! I cannot cross it, even if it *hurts them. This process heals me all over, especially in my heart." As I said this, I would put my head down and wipe a tear from my eye. I then would raise my head up and say, "This decision was not easy, but necessary."*

* * *

As those words came, I could tell that my story penetrated the lady's heart, and she, too, was healed through my experiences.

The lady said, "Cindy, your story is exactly what I needed to hear. I felt your pain, as it is the same as mine. I understand how your words were from your heart, as they touched my heart. You don't understand how much that helped me."

The lady was in awe as she identified with my story and now understood what she needed to do next. "Cindy, you didn't tell me I had to do anything or force me to do something your way. You supported me by sharing your experience, and I am grateful. Sometimes hope is found even in the darkest times, as long as one remembers to turn on the light."

* * *

As significant as the unconditional love my mother, Cindy, showed me was, the love I wanted to give my son but couldn't due to addiction was the same. This account is told so that other children whose loved ones are stuck in addiction are able to transform through this story and understand how important it is to love them when they don't know how to love themselves. It truly is no child, no parent, and no addict left behind.

I was trying to spend time with my son, Zavier, who was six. It appeared to be a lovely fall day with a father and son at the park, but behind this picture was the darkness of my addiction. He was having so much fun at the park, but it was a different story for me. I grabbed my head and screamed, "Will it ever shut off?"

My mind kept racing, and I could hear my addiction give orders loud and clear. "Joey, what do you think you're doing? You don't have any time for your son! I *need you*! Look here, Joey; you are on my time, not his! When I say march, you march. Am I clear?" I nodded my head and knew that my addiction was in charge.

"Daddy, I missed you," Zavier said quietly, grabbing my shirt as I pulled away, not letting my son see my tear. I started walking away from him, and I could hear the conversation between my son and my mother from a distance. "Grandma, what is wrong with my dad? He always has to leave when I come to see him. Is it something I did, or is something wrong with me?"

"No, Zavier, you're fine. Your father is sick, and we can only pray he gets better."

Zavier replied, "I don't want him to be sick; I just want him to love me."

My mother answered with a tear falling, "Zavier, he needs to learn how. This sickness is not the sick that you know. Just keep praying for him, Zavier." My son looked down, and a tear fell down his face as he grabbed my mother's hand tight and would not let go.

As I stood there, my mind was getting louder and louder. "Joey...

Joey...LISTEN UP!" The obsession and compulsion of my addiction were now yelling at me.

My eyes were wide open, and I answered my addiction, muttering, "I can hear you; I'm up, I know!" I looked at my son, who was distraught, and said, "Zavier, I have to leave now. I have to go. I am sorry."

"You always have to leave, Dad," Zavier replied as he started tearing up.

"Sorry, Zav. I need to go now. I'm sorry."

"Sorry" was a word we all knew too well. It was a word that was meaningless—so many promises, so many empty promises.

I stood there talking to myself, saying, "He probably doesn't know I can't stop using, right...right...heh. How can kids know, anyway?" I was sweating from the opiate withdrawal that kept me in a vicious cycle.

Zavier was tying his shoe. He started to get up and looked over at me as I walked away. I heard him say, "My dad is sick, so sick. Why can't he love me? Maybe he will get help one day; I hope he does. Please, God, help my dad."

The truth is that kids know when their parents use. I used, but my son suffered. They don't give up on us; they are always there, waiting to love us back to life.

In a recovery medicine world, there is always a way out and back to our family's heart. The journey is a challenging path, though, with many hills and valleys, each coming with a storm that can shake us up. Making sure to stay steadfast through the storms of life is what builds our character as we grow.

As an addict, I must not give up, ever. I need to remind myself that yes, I did use, and yes, my family suffered. But it didn't make me a bad person. I was a sick person needing to get well. There is always hope, and it is worth fighting for.

Hope was my inspiration, and hope was what kept me going. It was always about helping and being of service. I learned a long time ago that service is for those we serve, not us. Today I am a father and a practitioner. As a father, I need to set the example to be that vision of hope for my children and meet them where they are. As a practitioner, it is up to me to do the same. When harm reduction is all you have, it is up to me to light the way.

Chapter 9

WHEN HARM REDUCTION IS ALL YOU HAVE

Addiction has hurt so many families because of the stigma in our nation telling us how and when we need to recover. It is about meeting someone where they are and loving them through their process. When harm reduction is all you have, someone's self-determination must come first.

I was once asked how vital harm reduction is to me. To answer this question is to give you a part of me, as I have many stories of harm reduction; all have been powerful and life-changing. To answer the person's question, I had to take them back into my memories, which changed how I viewed harm reduction.

The days of the COVID-19 pandemic were a dark time in our country. It was when mental health and substance use disorders were isolated with no hope in sight. Behavioral health treatment was getting a makeover with a new modality of care called telehealth. However, the rural areas of southwestern Pennsylvania were full of disparities that led to increases in opiate overdoses. Governor Wolf and the rest of the Department of Human Services (DHS) were forced to act on implementing safety measures to protect the vulnerable populations of our state. Telehealth became a blessing in the storm, but it still needed to be modified in many areas. This was not a cookie-cutter method to treat persons with behavioral health disorders.

I was working as a care navigator, caseworker, certified recovery specialist (CRS), and recovering addict. I was on a mission to engage as many persons suffering from addiction as I could get into treatment and to try to make a difference. It was time to go out for mobile outreach to the rural parts of Greene County, the southwesternmost part of Pennsylvania, hoping for harm reduction. Before leaving, I sat in my car calling clients in my attempt to engage them first and see where they were. While I did this, another story was being told at the client's residence.

Outside a house in an isolated part of Greene County, you could hear the incessant barking of dogs. It was early morning on a spring day, and the lady looked at her husband with the same sadness she had carried for too long, saying, "Will we ever get out of this?"

"I don't know," he muttered. He then looked her in the eyes, hugged her tight, and said, "Dear, it's those moments when it's life or death, use or not, pain or suffering, decisions like that will determine the fate of our life, and possibly others."

"They have for years and years. It has to stop sometime!" She laid her head down and cried because she knew that addiction had them both in its grips and would not let go.

The man went to his desk in their home and saw his casework-er's business card and some empty Narcan packets.

He chuckled, saying to himself, "I told that caseworker I did not want that stuff...heh...but if I didn't have it, she would be dead." They could not go anywhere, as COVID-19 precautions were everywhere and they were stuck with no car and a government-subsidized phone, which barely had any cellular service in their neck of the woods.

This was the reality of what went on in the couple's house daily. I knew this, and it was why I must never give up. As I was still in the car making phone calls, the next number I dialed was the couple whom I just discussed. They were at the top of my list, as they were high-risk and had a history of overdoses. I picked up my phone and called them, hoping they might pick up the phone and engage this morning.

As I pressed the last number, the couple raised their heads when their phone rang, which the lady answered and then mumbled a soft hello.

It was apparent in her voice that addiction had broken her down to the point of no return. A new method of therapeutic services that used cellular devices of various kinds, called tele-health, had been the saving grace for this couple all through the pandemic. Neither of them was ready to be clean yet, but judging their desire was not up to me. Sometimes, I would make weekly telehealth phone calls that were the only form of harm reduction I had against the disease of addiction. This was as good as it got for people who were not ready to leave the pits of despair.

When I was talking to the couple, I made sure they knew that I was willing to meet them where they were, saying, "Listen, it's okay if you aren't ready to be clean. I am not here to tell you what to do. I am here for you when you are ready to make a change." I paused and said, "Let me at least drop off Narcan to you tomorrow." They both knew that I meant what I said and cared.

The client responded, "We don't need it!"

I then talked louder to ensure the couple knew how important this was to hear. "Didn't you tell me you used it on your wife last week when she overdosed?"

He nodded and said, "Yes."

"Well, take some, in case you need it again," I said with emphasis.

The client rolled his eyes with a smirk and replied, "Okay."

I could almost feel his apathy through the phone, but I knew that it was not about me, and harm reduction came in many forms. I paused, nodded, and said, "I'll drop it off in your mailbox so that I won't bother you."

I hung up the phone, looked up, and said to myself, "I remember when I was in their place and couldn't notice all the caring and love in the world. I was not ready, though I knew they were out there." If a person can look outside the box and see the many silver linings in the world, they might be able to change. What lays the foundation of a relationship is preserving principles such as the self-determination and autonomy of a person. It is not up to me to play God, no matter what my credentials say. If the only form of harm reduction is giving a person a lifesaving drug such as Narcan, then it is what I must do. I do not get to pick who lives and dies, who gets it, and who does not. Once again, if a person is not ready to change, I cannot say the right thing, but if they are, I cannot say the wrong thing.

In the weeks following my dropping off Narcan at the couple's house, they started calling me asking me to give them more, which I did weekly for the next three months.

One day the man called me and said, "Joey, I appreciate Narcan more than you know. I am sorry for being so ignorant in our past conversations. The disease of addiction still has me in its grips, and it won't let me go. I want to see about us coming in to get on Suboxone." Suboxone was a medication used in the MAT modality at our facility.

Two weeks later, the couple came in and decided to change their lives. They were put on Suboxone and wanted to start living and stop dying. I discussed the direction we were going with this case with my colleague, Dr. Scott Cook. This was an example of a case where clients agreed to some harm reduction after my persistence at their residence week after week.

Weeks later, the couple walked back into the facility, looking the best they ever had in years, but still unable to smile.

The woman looked at the physician and said, "Thank you, Dr. Cook."

A treatment plan was made for the clients to eventually taper off to an abstinence-based program, accompanied by twelve-step support and meetings.

As we talked with the couple, they interrupted Dr. Cook and me and said, "We appreciate all this help, but I don't understand why you did not give up on us. We made it so hard on you!"

Dr. Cook said, "We're not going to give up on you two. That's what this is all about."

She hugged me and he shook Dr. Cook's hand, as both had tears that they were trying to hold back. The couple then walked out of our office as the workday ended.

As more time passed, the couple walked into the facility smiling as they encountered the staff. They were both tapering down on their medications while preparing for an abstinence-based treatment plan that was somewhat of a dream a year prior.

The man looked at me and said, "You respected my wishes and waited until I was ready to change. I can see that you and Dr. Cook care rather than telling me what I need to do."

I then looked at the couple and told them, "Listen, it's the old act of 'helping you helps me' or 'pain shared, pain lessened.'" I never know when I may help somebody, but I know that it is one of the best ways to connect with them. So, in a sense, empathy is finding echoes of another addict in myself; therefore, I know now that I am not unique, but just another addict on this journey called recovery.

Moments like watching a person grow from a minimal type of

harm reduction to MAT and then to abstinence-based treatment genuinely are unforgettable. I know that God is speaking to me through a vessel and telling me that if I listen and share my feelings, not only will I get better, but the hearts who feel my pain will also heal. Those unguarded moments before and after my storms are all that recovery is to me. It's all about buckling up, learning to hold on, and not using *no matter what* when the storms of life pass by.

This story demonstrates what love, compassion, and empathy are all about. It is about not giving up on someone and meeting someone where they are. Harm reduction is not only vital but a practitioner's way of life. Just as it was important to meet that couple where they were in their choice of treatment, so is a parent meeting a child where they are. My parents wanted me to be clean on their time, as my father would say, "Why can't you just get clean now?" I still had more pain to learn from, and it almost cost me my life. Though, no matter how bad it got, I needed to face it. Many times, overdosing almost took me out of this world.

A mother's experience of her son's overdose is something that no parent should ever have to endure. When harm reduction is all you have, it is something that, when witnessed, can change the course of your life forever. The following story is told by my mother, Cindy, who can help other parents see how it has to be enough when harm reduction is all you have.

* * *

If it weren't for harm reduction, I would not have a son today. Heroin almost took him from me, and I thank God that he's still alive every day.

I was sitting on my porch swing as the sun was starting to set on a warm summer night. I conversed with my son until he began to nod, and then he collapsed on the ground.

Shaking him, I yelled, "Joey...Joey! Wake up! WAKE UP! Why won't you move?" His lips turned blue. I cried out to my husband, "Tim, call 911 now! NOW!" Tears rushed down my face, and I attempted to use my phone, but my hand shook as I tried to push the buttons to call for help. I dropped my phone and screamed, "Don't...LEAVE...ME!" I didn't know how to perform CPR or tell if he was even breathing. He grabbed my arm and would not let go of me. The neighbors ran from next door, wondering what was happening while my son lay there motionless, now gasping for breath. I got on my knees beside him and prayed as I always did, yelling, "Take me, God, take me! Let him live! YOU CAN'T HAVE HIM!" The neighbor grabbed me, but I tried to break free when the paramedics arrived and took Joey into the ambulance, checking his pulse.

I was taken away from the scene as he was being worked on, though I could hear the paramedics talking during the commotion.

"Another overdose?" the EMT said. "Yeah, imagine that," the paramedic replied. "Just keep giving him Narcan doses; I'm sure he'll wake up and yell at us. He'll tell us that we ruined his high. Maybe he will go to treatment, maybe," said the nurse.

The paramedic looked at the EMT and put his hand on her shoulder, saying, "Yes, we can only pray." After three doses of Narcan, the blue lips that Joey had were regaining their color as he started sweating and moving around. He came to, and it was visible that chills were going down his spine as he continued to arch his back.

As the Narcan took effect, he was in complete opiate withdrawal and didn't know what had happened. My son looked up at the paramedic and did his best to talk as his stomach dropped, and he was still sweating profusely.

He was about to yell at the paramedic for putting him back into opiate withdrawal, but the EMT grabbed his hand and said, "You're lucky to be alive, kid."

"Heh, I guess so," Joey stated with remorse.

"Ma'am, your son has track marks all over his arms; he must have been using heroin for quite some time," the paramedic told me.

"Is he alive? IS HE?" I asked.

"Yes, ma'am, he is," replied the nurse.

I then got on my knees, looked up to the sky, crying, and said, "Thank you." After some time, my son could walk and I hugged him, looking into his eyes and saying, "I won't give up on you."

That situation almost killed me that day. I believe in harm reduction and feel that it is vital to anyone suffering from addiction.

Narcan saved my son's life that day and is a lifesaving tool I believe in. When harm reduction is all I have as a mother, I must not give up, no matter what. My son did not get clean that day or a year later, but instead, he was given a harm reduction drug that saved his life; the seeds of hope were planted that day, I feel. Today, as a mother, I keep Narcan in my house and in my purse in case of an emergency.

How can I judge someone's desire? I did not tell my son that day that I would give up on him; rather, I hugged him and said, "I won't give up on you." Harm reduction comes in many forms, but as parents, it is not up to us to play God and have a cookie-cutter process for everyone trying to recover. It is all about love. Besides love, I learned many things in the process of being a mother with a child stuck in active addiction. For many years, I needed solutions because I didn't know what to do. How do I love him and not hurt him? I didn't want to leave him behind, but he was taking me down, and the pain worsened.

Chapter 10

SOLUTIONS FROM A RECOVERY MEDICINE WORLD

After looking at harm reduction, a person might wonder how someone can help and not hurt a person who is lost in the pits of despair. Whether they are addicts, family members, friends, or practitioners, one thing is for sure: they need to be loved. With addiction, regardless of treatment, if someone isn't ready to stop using, I can't say the right thing, but if they are, I can't say the wrong thing.

Addiction leaves us in a quandary. What do we do? What do we say? How do we do it? There are so many questions with no clear-cut answers. From a clinician's perspective, we make our best evidence-based decisions. Regarding answers, we can separate the perspectives: social work, family, and medical solutions.

This chapter is about the solutions to those questions brought up by my life experiences, whether personal or professional. It is broken up into social work, family, and medical solutions.

This chapter does not give any cookie-cutter process for everyone; instead, it is a basis that lights the way in our clinical and medical practices. Since recovery is individualized, it is up to the reader to know whether a solution would work for them. I address the social work and family sections while Dr. Cook covers the medical solutions. In the social work section, I present data-driven research that I have done, along with coauthors Janice McCall, LSW, PhD, and Jessica Morrow, MSW. Dr. Scott A. Cook will provide the medical solutions from his first-person perspective.

SOCIAL WORK SOLUTIONS

When it comes to an addict, recovery does not come easy. As a licensed clinician, my theoretical orientation is built on the systems theory framework. Looking at a person using that lens, I can see how to consider many factors of their life. I can address an addict's behavior in terms of multilayered relationships and environments. I can then conceptualize how their life is based on a person's needs, rewards, expectations, and attributes of the people living in the system. Therefore, there is not one "best" solution.

For a continuing treatment plan to be efficacious, I cannot send someone to inpatient treatment to get clean and send them back to the same toxic environment that fueled the addiction. Holistically, housing is just as important as therapy. Stability in each part of their life is connected to stability in the whole. There is not one solution for a person, but many, all necessary to maintain their recovery.

As a licensed social worker, my experience has been based on what is best for the client as observed and deemed necessary for harm reduction. In a clinical world, we are forced to see what works for a client and what does not. In substance abuse treatment, evidence-based programs are the future, such as the Centers of Excellence (COE).

* * *

While working at Southwestern Pennsylvania Human Services (SPHS), I evaluated how persons with opiate use disorder were impacted during the pandemic in a project called "Maintaining Client Satisfaction in Behavioral Health Services during COVID-19: Practice Implications for Telehealth." This is a published article in which I was the lead author, along with Janice McCall and Jessica Morrow. The project covered a medically underserved area (MUA) that needed to continue care for individuals currently in treatment, at higher risk of relapse and crisis, and at a geographic disadvantage when seeking healthcare and behavioral healthcare services.

One of the questions I had to ask myself was this: "What is the efficacy of telehealth, and does it help persons suffering from substance use disorder (SUD) or opiate use disorder (OUD) when we have major barriers such as the pandemic preventing face-to-face care for our clients?"

I saw the significance of their lack of stability during these dark times. It was the pandemic and we were utilizing telehealth services, which was a blessing in the storm as I saw it. However, their efficacy needed to be measured. We formed our study around telehealth services among COE clients formerly accessing in-person behavioral healthcare services in our rural community during the early transitions to telehealth service delivery due to COVID-19.

According to Pagano et al., "Survey respondents included 100 clients (43 males and 57 females) at two Southwestern Pennsylvania behavioral health provider program locations who were actively accessing in-person behavioral health services pre-COVID-19 and then continued care via telehealth when COVID-19 precautions prevented clients from in-person sessions. Despite a minority of clients responding that they did not get as much out of telehealth services as they did from face-to-face services ($N = 13$), the level of satisfaction among those who did get as much out of telehealth services ($N = 87$) was substantive ($\phi = .48$). Findings suggest participants perceived an equitable clinical experience when comparing their past face-to-face behavioral health care services to telehealth" (2022; see www.ship.edu/globalassets/keystone-journal/v8n1_pagano_morrow_mccall.pdf).

Another important finding from our study suggests a successful perceived transfer of the quality of the therapeutic relationship between the practitioners and their clients. One aspect of this study's host organization (SPHS) is its commitment to developing a strong therapeutic rapport with its clients.

Rapport is defined as a close and harmonious relationship in which the people or groups concerned understand each other's feelings or ideas and communicate well (see https://bit.ly/3WrOYUQ). Whether the client is in inpatient, outpatient, medication-assisted, or abstinence-based treatment, rapport with the clinician bridges the gap with the client being able to remain stable.

The SPHS COE has been the vehicle for delivering service continuity and client satisfaction for persons trying to recover from OUD while maintaining their treatment. Its vision is "to ensure individuals in the community with opioid use disorder receive individualized, integrated treatment for their addiction, behavioral health, and physical needs. This is accomplished by utilizing a multidisciplinary team of individuals in recovery with life experience and substance abuse professionals trained in trauma-informed care" (SPHS, 2022; see www.sphs.org).

As data has shown, there is not a one-size-fits-all treatment modality for every client. When meeting a client where they are, there needs to be a broad range of treatments for the growing OUD population. Telehealth has become the service modality that will likely continue for its ease of access, efficiency, and immediacy of care (Pagano et al., 2022).

Not only has the SPHS COE been data-driven, but it has also helped over 3,750 clients engage in some form of substance use treatment since its inception in 2017. OUD programs such as this have helped stabilize the client in inpatient, outpatient, and various medication-assisted treatment modalities by linking the clients to these vital services.

The COE staff are available for referrals from anyone and respond to an opioid crisis 24/7. The COE staff can respond in person in the community. They can facilitate warm hand-offs from the emergency department to treatment services, from services to nontreatment recovery support services, or between levels of care for treatment. During the referral process, demographics and substance abuse history are obtained. Once an individual is deemed appropriate by having an opioid use diagnosis, the team develops strategies to engage that individual and begins assessing for individualized treatment and nontreatment needs. An initial trauma-informed assessment is completed to gather social determinants of health, substance abuse, physical health, and behavioral health history.

The assessment guides referrals to obtain an American Society of Addiction Medicine (ASAM) level of care through a substance abuse treatment provider, which includes the following levels of care: Medically Managed Intensive Inpatient Services, Medically Monitored Intensive Inpatient Services, Clinically Managed High-Intensity Residential Services, Clinically Managed Population-Specific High-Intensity Residential Services, Clinically Managed Low-Intensity Residential Services, Residential/Inpatient Services, Partial Hospitalization Services, Intensive Outpatient Services, Intensive/Partial Hospitalization Services, and Outpatient Services.

Medication-assisted treatment options are discussed during the assessment, including induction of buprenorphine, methadone, and naltrexone. In addition, the agency has protocols and processes to ensure all individuals are provided with education regarding the risks and benefits of medication-assisted treatment and overdose risks, along with providing immediate access to naloxone and naloxone education. The COE offers the induction of naltrexone within twenty-four hours of the individual's agreement to an evaluation.

Regardless of one's treatment journey, there are many paths that a person can choose. In a recovery medicine world, theoretically, the solution might make sense; clinically, it might not.

Social work solutions look at what works and what doesn't but also make sure to value the person's self-determination.

FAMILY SOLUTIONS

As vital as social work solutions are to the stability of a person seeking recovery, a family almost always, in some capacity, becomes collateral damage from the disease of addiction. Even though one person uses substances, the family of the addict also requires healing. Whether a parent or a child, each family member plays an essential role in helping that person get as healthy as they can. There is not one set solution for every using addict. The hardest pill to swallow is knowing this statement to be true: "If the person is not ready to quit, then love is not enough." Love is a double-edged sword that a using addict can manipulate into their destruction. You simply cannot keep someone clean if they do not want it. A person's addiction is more powerful than their recovery. It is stronger than a child's or parent's love.

Clinically, it makes no sense, and I cannot want it more than they do. My mother used to pray for me and wanted me to be clean so badly, yet I did not get clean until I was ready. I'm sure many people who read this book know someone they want to get clean, but they have no choice but to watch from the sidelines while that person is slowly killing themselves. This is the bitterness of addiction. I cannot love someone clean, for love has become a weapon that can be forged in many ways.

My father always said to me, "Just quit." But I would say, "Dad, I wish I could, and it was that easy." An excellent solution to help a child is to love them and not enable them. To enable their child is to let them run all over their parents' hearts while dragging them through the mud. Yet, there is no cookie-cutter process when it comes to love. Some people stay clean while their parents love and enable them throughout their active addiction. This is something that only a parent will know when they are done. Parents with children in active addiction are like a ticking bomb waiting to go off, without knowing how to put out the fuse. There are various support groups for families of using addicts. This support helps put out the fuse before it is too late. Parents need to talk and see that they are not the only ones suffering.

An example of a time when love was not enough to keep that person clean is on a trip I made to the local hospital.

It was 5:00 p.m. on a Thursday, and I was being wheeled on a gurney into the ER of the same hospital where my mother once worked for years. I had some minor chest pains that were stress-induced, which I did not know at the time.

As I entered the room, there were nurses, a doctor, and other medical staff. A woman came up to me with deep purple eyes that pierced into my heart as she talked. "Joey, Joey Pagano? You are Joey Pagano, correct?" I did not know how to respond, for I was surprised by her approach. I spoke up and said, "Yes, what's going on?" She grabbed my hand as the rest of the room went silent. Her grip tightened, and she said, "You helped me get through my son's death. You tried many times to help him, but he was not ready. You helped me understand how to love him from a distance."

As a tear ran down her face, everyone in the room looked at us, and she said, "I can never repay you." I smiled at her and said, "You don't have to repay me." She smiled and said, "Through talking to you and your mother, I understood what you meant. You said, love alone cannot keep him clean. Though that statement hurt me, I knew you spoke the truth, Joey. Thank you, and God bless you." She walked away, and I was able to leave the ER soon.

That is the sad truth when it comes to addiction; there isn't a perfect solution all the time. In my experience, love can help but also hurt someone simultaneously.

There is not a one-size-fits-all solution for a family member who is using. Sometimes all we can do is love them from a distance. Other times, we hold their hand while we help them learn to love themselves again. Either way, we must support that family member while they practice discernment with their loved one, and not enable them. Otherwise, we aren't helping them; we are hurting them.

So, as a parent, a child, a recovering addict, and a clinician, it is up to me to not enable a family member and to look for warning signs. Some of these are, but are not limited to, poor hygiene, sleeping too much, having track marks on their arms, constantly asking for money and not having anything to show for it, or nodding out in conversation. Once some of these behaviors are noted, it is a good idea to talk to the family member and see what they say. Talk to others who might be well versed in substance abuse issues. If there is a Center of Excellence in your area, they could help. In southwestern Pennsylvania, the SPHS COE has a toll-free number that takes referrals 24/7, which is 1-888-810-8595.

The COE uses people in recovery, which can bridge gaps that might be needed for that person seeking recovery. The worst thing to do is rationalize and justify their behavior, which can help send that person to an early grave. The stigma of "not my child" has kept many people from knowing about recovery. We must, as a family, leave no addict behind.

MEDICAL SOLUTIONS

After looking at family solutions, medical solutions are the last pieces of the puzzle. This part is best told by Dr. Scott A. Cook. It is told in his first-person perspective to give the reader a closer look at his background related to many years of recovery medicine practice.

Over the years, as we understand more about substance use disorders, medical terminology has changed. Previously, we used terms like "abuse" versus "dependence." The thought back then was that some people were just abusing substances but not totally addicted, while others were dependent upon the substance and truly addicted. This old terminology has fallen by the wayside because it insinuated that people abusing substances were doing better than those dependent. Even though there is some truth to this, current terminology encourages providers to use the all-inclusive term "substance use disorder" (SUD).

The COVID-19 pandemic has had an impact on the prevalence of substance use. The isolation associated with the pandemic increased substance use disorders, particularly with alcohol. Additionally, with advances in technology like online ordering, individuals could purchase alcohol and have it delivered to their homes.

Various treatment recommendations are available for common substances of abuse, including alcohol, opiates (heroin, fentanyl, carfentanyl, prescription pain pills, kratom), stimulants (cocaine, methamphetamine, MDMA/ecstasy), benzodiazepines, hallucinogens (phencyclidine [PCP], LSD [acid], mushrooms, peyote), other designer drugs (bath salts, China White, gammahydroxy butyrate [GHB]), prescription drugs (opiates, stimulants, gabapentin), other prescription sedative hypnotics (sleeping pills), nicotine, anabolic-androgenic steroids, caffeine, and inhalants.

The use of various substances can cause multiple physical and mental problems. Some issues arising from substance use include oropharyngeal cancer, gastrointestinal cancer, pancreatitis, breast cancer, lung cancer, hepatitis, seizures, cirrhosis, skin infection, blood infection (sepsis), soft tissue infection, bone infection, HIV, other infectious diseases, nasal septum perforation, cardiovascular disease, heart attack, sudden cardiac death, hypertension, severe psychiatric disease, extreme sedation, mental health changes, vital sign instability, and death. Medication-assisted treatment (MAT) is available for some substances, including prescriptions to decrease cravings, eliminate use, treat mental health diseases, and provide symptom relief/comfort.

We are hearing in the news that death from suicide, substance use, and despair are on the rise. Substance use increases the likelihood of poor mental health, despair, addiction, and suicide. Anne Case and Angus Deaton first wrote about "deaths of despair"—deaths by suicide, drug use, and alcohol poisoning.

The lifetime prevalence rate for all mental health disorders is 30 to 50 percent. This means that 1 in every 2 or 3 people you encounter has, had, or will have a mental health condition at some point in their lifetime. *Diagnosis and treatment of mental health problems are of vital importance, and prevention is of paramount importance.*

US Congress Joint Economic Committee report on September 5, 2019, stated mortality from deaths of despair far surpasses anything seen in America since the dawn of the twentieth century.

Long-Term Trends in Deaths of Despair (Source: Social Capital Project analyses of CDC data). The co-occurrence of substance use and mental health disorders shows significant overlap. Many people use substances to self-medicate undiagnosed mental health conditions. Likewise, many people who have been formally diagnosed with mental health conditions end up getting addicted to substances.

Many factors play into the development of a substance use disorder. Furthermore, the existence of previous life trauma significantly contributes to substance use. Repeated physical and mental trauma can cause literal or figurative numbness. In terms of mental numbness, this escape is comforting to a patient who has suffered previous trauma. Substance use contributes to creating comforting numbness. Therefore, it is easy to see why historical trauma increases the risk of developing an addiction.

Not only is mental health a central issue in substance use, but the social determinants of health (SDOH) also play a role. SDOH contribute to substance use while also being a barrier preventing people from getting adequate treatment (Source: Kaiser Family Foundation: Beyond Health Care: The Role of Social Determinants in Promoting Health and Health Equity [May 10, 2018]).

The reasons people end up using substances are truly multifactorial. Historical trauma, mental health conditions, and family history of mental illness or substance use, along with social determinants of health, all play a part. We certainly must eliminate the stigma associated with substance use and treat patients suffering from addiction with competence and compassion.

The medical standpoint that Dr. Cook discusses is just as important as the social work and family solutions. We are on the same team, fighting for our patients, clients, families, and ourselves and hoping our empathy and compassion can buy some time. It is always about not giving up on the person and continuing to meet them where they are, rather than where the social worker, loved one, or practitioner is. Overall, recovery medicine is an individualized process, where regardless of the modality or treatment desired, the goal is no person left behind.

Chapter 11

NO ADDICT LEFT BEHIND

After looking at the various solutions that this book focuses on, the shared theme surrounding them has been that no addict be left behind. Hope is the only principle that we can give a person. It is about not giving up on someone, no matter what, and when that is done, it gives someone hope.

Hope is sometimes expressed through the lens of memories that touch someone's heart. This book has touched on so many things that helped me as a brother, husband, son, father, clinician, and recovering addict grow as a person. As I grew, I learned how vital giving someone your time is. To me, that's what life is about. It is about giving people grace, showing love, and being able to listen to their hearts while not judging them from the outside. It is about putting away our implicit biases and prejudices about who they are and what they do and loving them right where they are, unconditionally.

This chapter contains four stories that are all about how no addict is left behind. Together, the stories concentrate on all of the chapter titles and are about accepting an addict for where they are rather than where the person is and not judging them.

The first story tells a tale of compassion, empathy, and love. These three principles are vital to helping a person break free of the stigmatized thinking that holds them hostage in their mind.

As I walked into a client's house, I glanced at their luggage next to the door. I sat down and asked the person, "Are you going somewhere?"

He bowed and said, "No, I'm not, Joey."

"Okay, well, why is it there?" I asked.

He raised his head, and a tear fell down as he said to me, "Joey, I keep it there because I know I will go to treatment soon enough. I've been there twenty-five times and it just does not make sense to unpack since I know I will eventually return when I have enough pain."

I hugged him and said, "I am not going to give up on you, no matter what." He believed me and though he didn't have enough faith in himself, he knew that I believed in him and that was enough hope to get him by.

Looking through the lens of physical health, a situation like that would clinically not make sense. The sad thing is that the wounds of stigma from physical health are not as deep as recovery medicine. As a practitioner, you must be that last person standing, that last line of defense, when the rest of the world has given up on them because you are the *hope*. Walking into an emergency room or an ambulance, the stigma is so alive that sometimes it keeps a person from getting help, even when needed. I had many conversations with professionals in that field, and I did not blame them for how they felt. The National Association of Social Workers (NASW) (2022) states, "Social workers pursue social change, particularly with and on behalf of vulnerable and oppressed individuals and groups of people." As a social worker, I must serve in the trenches, pulling people out and not giving up on them. We live in a world where the vulnerable populations of persons with SUD and OUD face barriers and need support. Balancing a person's self-determination and not enabling them is very difficult and can harm them or help them.

That same self-determination I had for a client, my family had for me. The second story reflects on that theme and loves me where I am. This experience involves my sister, Samantha, and my mother, Cindy. There isn't a day that goes by when I do not thank God for gracing me with these angels, for they were divine appointments that I did not see coming. It was a dark time in my life; very few stayed around and continued to let me walk over them. My sister would not give up but had to keep a distance from me, protecting herself.

She loved me so much that she would do anything I asked. I overdosed so many times that she lost count. It was at a point where Sam could only mutter, "So be it." These words reflected her giving up and accepting that I would die soon, though she always had some hope that one day I would get clean.

My mother also stayed optimistic that I would make it, though she and my sister were the only ones with this mentality. My sister was wiser and knew that my addiction was too toxic for her. Sam had to be the strong one when it came to me.

My sister would wonder what it would take for my mother to distance herself from me as she did. Sam would say, "Mom, let him go! He is killing you and our family! What is it going to take?"

My mom worked in the local hospital, and some other mothers with children in addiction would consult her for advice and support. She made her peace by trusting that God had a plan for her son; no matter what, she would never give up.

As time went on, she would learn how not to enable me yet love me from a distance. I would never be given money, leading to more substance use. I would try to manipulate her, but a line had to be drawn, and I would not pass, no matter what. For any parent, loving a child can mean different things to different people. Though, when dealing with addiction, it's another type of monster.

Cindy said, "I am never giving up, but they...they...will have to find their way. This is so hard! I need to hold on and trust that what will happen will happen."

You can feel the ambiguity in her words as they were expressed daily with tears.

My mother yelled, "As long as I hold on, maybe he could find his way to be okay!"

Little did she know that my distorted perspective of happiness was all I knew. My addiction left me emotionless, which was shared with my mother as she seemed to have been stuck in time while chained to my heart.

My mother would say, "He had me lost and I knew I could only achieve happiness by letting him go, but that is something that was so hard to do, no matter what. I want him to be okay, not to feel any more pain, and be okay."

Cindy knew deep inside that I had to feel some pain; if not, I might not change. I think that sometimes pain changes us. In these moments, we either go or grow through it. She knew that enabling me had left her sick, and what had to be done first was self-love. The day my mother started living and stopped dying was when she could accept my condition and not leave it behind.

At that moment, she quit being afraid of what could go wrong and got excited about all the things that could go right. Regarding not giving up on a person, I think of the principle of reciprocity. I try to live my life in a program in which that principle holds true. It is an expression of getting true freedom when it is applied. It is true that if I want to give out hate, I will most likely get it back tenfold; hate is too big of a burden to carry anyway. When I do not let go of things, I believe I miss blessings by remaining stuck. It is a fundamental way of life and the exact principle on which I try to base my life.

My recovery is a reciprocal experience: I get out of it what I put into it, I reap what I sow, people treat me the way I treat them, and the way I live determines the way I live. This same logic is what we must have to not give up on someone. Even in the darkest moments, I must turn on the lights to get hope.

Loving someone from a distance is not giving up on them; instead, it is a form of protection. It is necessary for the person's stability. As human beings, we all have dark moments, but if we gave up on someone every time they had one of those moments, what kind of friend would we be?

The third story is about a person I would not give up on, even in the darkest moments of her life. I was at a crossroads with a client whom everyone else had given up on except me.

I was at her residence, trying to engage her and trying to give her some hope. We were in her living room as she sat in her recliner, dope sick while sweat poured off her face.

She looked up at me, saying, "Why do you constantly not give up on me? I have yelled at you, ran, and have not given you any reason to continue to help me. Yet, you still are there for me, even in my worst times. You also will not help unless I do my part, which makes me meet you halfway every time. Joey, I just do not understand."

I looked at her and said, "Come with me and let me show you something." She looked up and stared into my eyes, still shaking from the dope sickness. She got into my car and we went back to my office, where I went over to my desk and grabbed a hemp bracelet lying there. I put it in her hand and said, "This bracelet was the first piece of hope I was given on one of many attempts at staying clean."

A tear ran down her face as she smiled, showing that she felt those words. I said, "Listen, this was hope to me when I was ready to give up; I couldn't get it. I could not stay clean. The overdoses were getting worse and worse. I believe that I went to rehab the day before I would die."

I looked up at the client, saying, "Let me show you what hope feels like." I started telling her the story of a time when I went to rehab.

It was the day I got to the facility, and as I walked in I saw a man sitting on the floor making bracelets. I glanced over at him and was still emotionless while beginning to detox from the opiates. Part of me still wanted to leave and not be there, so my mind felt like a battlefield; at the time, I was not winning.

The man spoke up and said, "Hey, I am glad you are here; we have been waiting for you."

I gasped and replied, "What do you mean, you were waiting for me? You didn't even know I was coming."

As I walked toward the door, the man said, "Hey, come here."

I walked toward him to see what he wanted. My chills were getting worse throughout my body as I detoxed, and I could barely hold my head up.

"Hold out your hand," he whispered. I was the only one who could hear him.

As I held out my hand, he gave me a hemp bracelet and closed my fingers over it while I looked into his eyes.

He said, "You can do this, for I believe in you!"

Those words penetrated my heart without my permission and gave me a sense of hope that I did not have before. This was a defining moment in my life that had me thinking someone believed in me when I didn't believe in myself. That bracelet I took with me throughout my journey, and in it were those feelings of hopelessness. It was a symbol of perseverance that I never could lose.

Back in my office, my client now understood what hope was. The client then stated that she knew the meaning behind "we must never give up." She realized that my journey was built from my hard-won experiences, making me into who I am now. She said softly, "Joey, I now know why you truly believe that statement, we must never give up on anyone, no matter what."

I replied, "Yes! Because maybe that person will stay clean the twenty-sixth time. If we gave up on them on the twenty-fifth time in treatment, they would not make it. Some people might disagree with my logic, but for me, it will always be no addict left behind."

Ask yourself: Do we still love our parents after they hurt us and continue to use? Or do we still love our children when they break us and continue to use? These are the questions we must ask ourselves when facing the decision to go or to grow. Some of them do not have anyone else left. How do we turn our backs and give up on the ones who need us the most? That addict needs us so much from any distance, and they have chosen to love us. If we leave them, where do we leave them, and at what time and with whom? When hope is all they have, we must not leave them behind.

Some moments just like that story have made me into who I am today. It gave me hope the same way my loved ones do. My daughter, Gianna, is another vision of hope to me who never gives up, no matter what. The fourth and final story is one about my daughter. It is about me setting an example at my home of no addict left behind.

As I was getting home from work one day, I walked into my house and saw my daughter standing there.

Gianna walked up to me and hugged me, and said, "I'm proud of you."

I told her thanks and then asked her why she said that.

She looked at me and said, "I am proud of you because you help everyone, and I believe you have a good heart." I replied, "Listen, Gianna, I will pass and leave this world one day. But while I am here, I want to try to help save as many lost souls as possible. I want to make a difference so my kids can see my purpose."

"I understand why you do what you do. If you didn't help all those people, no one would. Dad, you don't leave people behind, no matter what. You never give up, ever. Even though I am your stepdaughter, you treated me just like your daughter. You love me unconditionally and I didn't get left behind. One day with you, I will meet your son. He will get to see what I see in you. You're not broken, Dad; you were never broken. You just needed to be repaired." At that moment, she hugged me, looked into my eyes, and said, "Dad, I'll never leave you behind."

Addicts are children, fathers, mothers, brothers, sisters, wives, husbands, and, most of all, human beings who deserve love and grace. It is up to us as practitioners, family members, and everyone else to not leave them behind. The stigma and dogma of addiction have killed many struggling people; it is up to us to pave the way. If you cannot love someone, then at least do not hurt them. In a recovery medicine world, there must be no addict left behind.

CONCLUSION

The stories told throughout this book encompass my viewpoint and those of my mother, Cindy Pagano; my father, Timothy Pagano; my wife, Jodie Pagano; my sister, Samantha Showman; my brother, Xavier Pagano; my son, Zavier Pagano; my daughter, Gianna Koget-Waddell; and Dr. Scott A. Cook. All of our perspectives on the various situations, whether family, social work, clinical, or medical, shared a common theme: "no addict left behind."

I sometimes ask myself where we draw the line between enabling and supporting. When does our last statement with our loved one become "Well, so be it"? As a provider, when do we discharge the client and know in our heart that we can't clinically help them anymore? We can safely say, "They need a higher level of care."

As friends, we say, "I have to love them from a distance." They become a "spiritual vampire" to us and suck the love right out of us. Do we give up? Is that even the right word for that situation? Are we really giving up, or are we protecting ourselves? Are these actions playing God, or are they discernment?

According to the Urban Dictionary (2022), enabling is "shielding a person from the consequences of a destructive behavior; allowing a person's destructive behavior to persist by managing or minimizing the ill effects of the behavior." Regardless of my role, my job is to help instead of hurting the person or client.

If addiction is a family disease and, in the end we all suffer, then is it safe to say we must protect ourselves first? While traveling the world working in the clinical field of recovery medicine, I have been put in situations where I had to choose whether to give up or not give up on someone. In long-term recovery, it is easier not to give up but harder to discern when to walk away. No matter what the situation presents, it all comes down to love. Whether the person is an addict or not, as human beings, it is our job just to be kind. And most of all, not to leave any person behind.

ABOUT THE AUTHOR

JOEY PAGANO is a social worker who has dedicated his life to the betterment of persons struggling with addiction. He is a loving husband, father, son, brother, and, most of all, recovering addict. He is the author of three books and continues to be of service to all in some capacity.

With Much Love And Appreciation

This book was written to pardon the recipient of any of your past transgressions. You are now free to heal. I also sign this book with the utmost pleasure and honor to this amazing person who stands before me.

_____

RECIPIENT

_____

PARDONER

Made in the USA
Las Vegas, NV
02 December 2023

81989728R00080